Welcome to
The Father's House

Bringing the Lord's Prayer to Life
through Story and Study

Kathy Bricel and Kathy Myers

Living a Spirit Led Life Bible Studies
Spirit Life Press

WELCOME TO THE FATHER'S HOUSE
Bringing the Lord's Prayer to Life through Story and Study

Front cover leaf illustration by Sandy Bricel Miller
Layout by Invisible Ink

Published by Spirit Life Press
PO Box 446
Yakima, WA 98907

ISBN 978-0-9833934-0-5
Printed in the United States of America
2011

Table of Contents

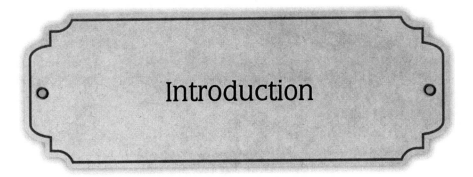

Introduction

Looking at the prayer Jesus shared with his disciples, we are given the secrets to living in relationship with the heavenly Father, our Father. Just as Jesus often taught about his Father through stories, this workbook is written in story format followed by Scripture, teaching, and questions. May the Holy Spirit bring new and deeper insights as you journey through the Lord's Prayer.

> *Our Father in heaven,*
> *hallowed be your name,*
> *your kingdom come,*
> *your will be done*
> *on earth as it is in heaven.*
> *Give us today our daily bread.*
> *Forgive us our debts,*
> *as we also have forgiven our debtors.*
> *And lead us not into temptation,*
> *but deliver us from the evil one.*

—Matthew 6:9-13

USING THE EIGHT WEEK STUDY GUIDE

- Each week's study is divided into five lessons. Plan on completing one lesson each day so the insights you are gaining will have time to soak in and be applied to your life.

- Invite the Holy Spirit to reveal to you what Jesus is teaching his disciples. If you find yourself feeling wholly and utterly dependent on the Father, then you are on the right track.

- Take time to listen and reflect on what you read and hear. If you are new to hearing God's voice, be patient and allow time to hear from the Lord.

- This workbook is written to be an interactive tool. Prayer was never meant to be a one-way monologue, but a dialogue between God and his children—a conversation that draws us into relationship with the One who created us and loves us.

- Terms used in this study include:
  DIG DEEPER—Extra Scripture for those who have the time and desire to delve a little deeper
  KINGDOM LAB—A tool to encourage you to hear from and interact with God

THE STORY OF THE STORY

"While you were gone, did you get any fresh ideas for the Lord's Prayer study we're supposed to be writing?" Kathy Bricel asked soon after I returned from a two week trip to the Holy Lands.

"Not really. You'd think I might have since I probably stood right where Jesus taught the prayer to the disciples! But no, nothing yet."

"I have some possibilities," Kathy said, "but I think we'd better get together, pray about it, and start writing. It's already mid-July, and we

What is your plan, Lord? How do you want to open hearts and minds to all that is packed into the Lord's Prayer?

need to have this ready by September." A workbook/study guide on the Lord's Prayer was in the plans for the Bible study we led in our church.

It was early morning on the day Kathy and I were meeting when I finally sat down, quieted myself and asked, "What is your plan, Lord? How do you want to open hearts and minds to all that is packed into the Lord's Prayer?"

My mind was blank, and I seemed fresh out of ideas. But I waited. And soon, the most unusual thing happened: the beginning of a story came to mind. Feeling a little perplexed, I went ahead and wrote it down. "Why a story?" I thought.

Yet as I read it, the words on the notebook paper touched my heart and I wanted to know what happened next. But it was almost time for Kathy to come over, so I desperately prayed again, "Lord, I don't know why I am writing a story, but please, as I get ready for the day, give me an idea for the Lord's Prayer study!"

It is always a blessing to work on a project with Kathy, but as we sat down, I felt badly that I didn't have any inspiring ideas to contribute for the workbook. Kathy shared her thoughts and then asked what I had heard from the Lord.

"All I have is a story. And I have no idea how it fits in or what it's for. But that's all I heard this morning," I replied, feeling as if I should have gotten up earlier to have had more time.

"Well, go ahead. Read it to me," Kathy invited.

After hearing what I had written, Kathy said, "That's good. What happens next?"

I shrugged my shoulders and answered, "I have no idea. I see a couple of glimpses of how experiences at The Father's House might help the Lord's Prayer come alive, but that's it. And how does a story work into a Bible study?"

Let the story help open your eyes to the kingdom of God. Let it break new ground in your heart to receive the love of the Father.

Kathy thought for a minute and then suggested, "Perhaps the study questions are woven throughout the story."

"Maybe," I replied. "But it's a simple story. I don't know."

"Jesus told simple parables, but they had great impact." Kathy paused. "I say we go for it; a story is what we have." Her eyes lit up, and she grinned. "Looks like another adventure! Let's see what happens."

Week by week the story began to unfold. It was a simple story, interwoven with the profound Word of God.

Let the story help open your eyes to the kingdom of God. Let it break new ground in your heart to receive the love of the Father. And let the Bible and the Lord speak to you, right where you are in life. Listen to him. He is an amazing and often surprising God. Who would have guessed a story and a Bible study would go together?

—Kathy Myers

LEARNING TO HEAR GOD'S VOICE

In searching the Scriptures to learn how to live life like Jesus lived, we realized we needed a key—a key to living in close relationship with the Father. In fact, Jesus lived so closely to the Father, he only did what he saw his Father doing (John 5:19). But *how* did this work? *How* did Jesus actually see his Father while he was on earth? *How* did he know where his Father was directing him to go? *How* did he know whom he was to heal, and when to teach?

Perhaps the key is right there, in the first chapter of Mark:

> *Very early in the morning, while it was still dark, Jesus got up,*
> *left the house and went off to a solitary place, where he prayed.*
> —Mark 1:35

Many of us have learned to talk to God, but do we take the time to listen?

Is prayer the key? If so, why aren't more of us already living like Jesus lived? Millions of people pray! However, prayer, or communicating with God, consists of both talking and listening. Many of us have learned to talk to God, but do we take the time to listen? Is it even possible for us to hear from God personally? What does the Bible say?

> *My sheep listen to my voice;*
> *I know them, and they follow me*
> —Jesus' words in John 10:27

The Scripture does not say "some of the sheep"; it implies that all of the shepherd's sheep listen to his voice. It is in our make-up as *sheep* to listen to our Shepherd's voice. So why do many of us miss out on hearing God speak directly to us?

> *In Hawaii on a family vacation, my youngest son said, "Come underwater, Mom, and listen. You've got to hear this!" I went underwater and listened—waiting to hear what he had heard. The sounds were clear—unmistakable: whales were communicating. It was amazing.*
>
> *The rest of my family was playing in the waves, and after getting out of the ocean, I asked them, "Did you hear the whales?" Seeing them shake their heads "no," I realized that they had been right there and yet had not thought to be quiet and listen. The beauty of the sounds was available to them, but they were focused on other things.*
>
> —Kathy Bricel

Our bodies live in the natural realm, but there is a spiritual realm as well. Picture the spiritual realm being like underwater life. We cannot see with our eyes all that goes on beneath the water's surface, but we know there is a complex eco-system under there.

We were meant to live in both the natural realm and the spiritual realm—to be spiritually amphibious.

It is as if Jesus came to the surface of the water—the Word becoming flesh and dwelling among us (John 1:14)—and taught us about life underwater. He has given us the gift of the Holy Spirit so we can put on our spiritual diving gear and submerge beneath the surface. We were meant to live in both the natural realm and the spiritual realm—to be spiritually amphibious. We were meant to stop and listen to God—to hear him clearly while living in this world...wherever we are.

> *Now the Lord is the Spirit,*
> *and where the Spirit of the Lord is, there is freedom.*
> —2 Corinthians 3:17

Since the Lord is the Spirit, he will primarily communicate to us through spiritual means. Perhaps a phrase in Scripture stands out to us, words to a song come to mind, or something in nature reveals insights about God. We must learn to listen with our spirits, believing that because we are his children, we will hear from our Father.

The more we listen, the easier it is to discern God's voice.

In our personal journeys, we have learned that God speaks to our spirits with thoughts that are natural to us—no *thees* or *thous*—and his truth, encouragement, and direction always agree with his written Word, the Bible. The more we listen, the easier it is to discern God's voice.

What about those thoughts that go through our minds that seem to tempt us or put us down? If we hear something contrary to the truth taught in Scripture, then it is as if we are listening to the wrong spiritual radio station. We must switch the channel and not spend time listening to the lies of the enemy or the insecurities of our own flesh. We must know God's Word so we can replace the lies with truth.

Hearing God's voice through the Bible and prayer is a key to beginning to live more like Jesus lived. So open your Bible, listen for God, and learn to recognize his voice. Choose to believe God is already speaking to you. Believe you are greatly loved, and know your Father has something to say. Put on your spiritual diving gear—life under the surface is a great adventure!

Enjoy the journey—
Kathy and Kathy

WEEK ONE
Our Father

THE STORY BEGINS   I read the sign posted on the iron fence:

—THE FATHER'S HOUSE—
ALL ARE WELCOME

Maybe I'm welcome, but how am I supposed to get in? It's certainly not very inviting to have a gate you can't see. It must be here somewhere.

Driving around the magnificent estate, I once again scrutinized the fence for an opening. A wide flagstone walkway meandered through the well-kept gardens and seemed to lead to the mahogany and glass door of the mansion.

But where does the walkway begin? Have all my arrangements been pointless? Taking the time off work, finding a dog-sitter, changing my schedule, studying the two pages of Google Map directions to get to this out-of-the-way location—maybe it has been a waste of time and vacation days.

At least the drive had been refreshing. The countryside glistened with the sun's reflection on the spring leaves, and the sense of new life filled me with anticipation.

Why had it taken so long to follow up on the way God had personalized the Bible verse in Matthew? Reading the Bible wasn't an everyday occurrence for me, but for some reason, that day I needed something more than I knew I would get from the morning news. So, randomly I opened the Bible to Matthew 11, and verse 28 seemed to say to me:

Come to me, you who are weary and burdened, and I will give you rest.
Come anytime; come for awhile.
Come—your heavenly Father is waiting and watching for you.

Come anytime; come for awhile. Come—your heavenly Father is waiting and watching for you.

I had a sense this verse was an invitation to something. So I waited. I'm not sure why—I've never expected to hear from God before—but I prayed, "What, Lord? What do you mean?"

"Come to The Father's House" resonated in my mind. *What am I supposed to do? Go to church? No, that doesn't seem to make sense.*

During work the next day, I couldn't get that thought out of my mind. *If it isn't church, what is The Father's House?*

Later, at home, I got side-tracked by the usual news, dinner, dog-walking, and then TV. So it wasn't until later that night that I thought more about The Father's House.

I decided to try praying again, but all I seemed to hear was the wind scurrying around outside. So I picked up my Bible and started reading. I happened to come to Jesus' words in John 17:11 as he prayed for those who follow him:

I will remain in the world no longer, but they are still in the world, and I am coming to you.

When I read the words "still in the world," Google Maps came to mind. I enjoy investigating project locations our company is considering, as well as places my friends and family live. I guess it's a

If it isn't church, what is The Father's House?

little bit of an escape. So when I thought about Google Maps, I figured it was just another distraction. But as I kept reading, I couldn't shake the thought that a Google search had something to do with this.

I went to the computer and searched "Father's House Washington state." Up popped 375,000 entries! *This is going to be futile.* I opened several sites that didn't seem to relate to my nudge before I clicked on "The Father's House. Come anytime."

A simple website came up on the screen with the Scripture I had been reading:

> *Come to me, all you who are weary and burdened,*
> *and I will give you rest. Take my yoke upon you and learn from me,*
> *for I am gentle and humble in heart, and you will find rest for your souls.*
> *For my yoke is easy and my burden is light.*

The words "Come anytime; come for awhile" were there, too. This had to be it. Not much information was given, but still, I clicked on "Get directions." *Where in the state is this?* The set of instructions was long, but thorough. *Why not take a chance? Tomorrow I'll check my calendar.*

As I walked into work the next day, my curiosity about the website was still stirring in my thoughts. *Remember to see when you can take a few days off.*

"Taylor, I need to talk to you right away," my boss said on my way into the office. After putting my things on the desk, I walked down the hall. *What an unusual greeting from my normally calm boss.*

"The Kilpatrick project needs some major revisions, and soon!" my boss explained. "Could you be ready to go to San Diego on the early flight tomorrow? You've got what it takes to push things along more quickly than anyone else, and I want you to stay for as long as you're needed. I'll fill you in this morning, and you can take the afternoon off to get ready."

What could I say? My job as project manager was excellent, and these sudden travel plans came up every so often. They were certainly part of the job. The choice was not really mine.

While I was away, about all I seemed to hope for were vision and enough rest so I'd be decent to the others working on the assignment. And things weren't much different when I got back to town. In order to catch-up at work, I carried paper work home every night for a couple of

> *It really was in plain sight, but somehow I'd expected something different and had totally missed it before.*

weeks; and the thoughts about The Father's House were put on a shelf in the back of my mind.

It wasn't until I started to google "fall foliage Vermont" for a future vacation that I was reminded of The Father's House. The words "Father's House Washington state" came up on my screen as I typed in "fa…," and I stopped. *What happened? How did I let that slide? Tomorrow I'll be sure to look at my calendar.*

Finally I'd cleared some days on my schedule and I was coming (or was I going?) to The Father's House; lately it seemed I was just trying to keep up with life as it happened around me. But I'd done it. I was here, driving along the fence still looking for the gate. *Once more, slowly. Where can it be?*

I stopped on the road by a group of wispy trees to take a look. Yes, there it was. I hadn't been paying close enough attention. It really was in plain sight, but somehow I'd expected something different and had totally missed it before.

I wondered if the gate was locked, but I parked my SUV and went to check. There was a small oblong sign, "Come in." I tried the latch, opened the gate, stepped inside, and looked around.

"Welcome!" it appeared as if the man greeting me was the gardener. His smile was wide, his eyes kind, and his handshake warm. There was something about him that seemed familiar. *Is it his voice? Why do I feel as if I already know him?*

"Let me help you get your bag," he offered. "Your room is all ready for you." *How does he know I'm staying, or better-yet, who I am?*

"Why don't you head over to that maple tree and have a seat?" he invited, directing me with his eyes. "I'll unload your bag and have something for you to drink in just a few minutes."

Stretching my legs, I wandered around marveling at the landscaping—moss, rocks, fir trees, and wildflowers. It reminded me of walking on mountain paths and noticing the details of nature's beauty. The maple tree was just ahead and had comfy-looking chairs nestled under its branches.

Soon I was sipping lemonade with fresh strawberries and talking to the gardener. I told him how I ended up here and that I wasn't sure what to expect. But I had been working hard and needed a break. I had an unusual sense that God might be offering a different kind of rest than I knew about. I wanted to see.

"Well, you are in the right place," the gardener began. "It sounds as if you could be ready to begin the process of disentangling from the things that keep you from living a life of peace and joy." I nodded. "While you're here, you can be equipped with everything you need. A restful state of mind is available for you every day."

Sounds good, but this man doesn't know about my life, my job, or my responsibilities. Of course rest is possible on this beautiful estate where there aren't any worries.

"It's really about being in relationship with your Heavenly Father. He is the one who extends the invitation, 'Come to me.' Are you familiar with the Lord's Prayer?"

> *I had an unusual sense that God might be offering a different kind of rest than I knew about. I wanted to see.*

"Sure," I answered. "We say it whenever I go to church."

"It holds the answers to being in relationship with God and to living in the peace of Christ. Why don't you walk around and see the grounds? I'll meet you back here in half an hour, after I've checked on a few things. By the way, Taylor, I'm Josh. And I look forward to our time together."

"Josh?" I glanced away. "Hmm, that's my father's name."

REFLECT

Our Father

Our Father in heaven,
hallowed be your name,
your kingdom come,
your will be done
on earth as it is in heaven.
Give us today our daily bread.
Forgive us our debts,
as we also have forgiven our debtors.
And lead us not into temptation,
but deliver us from the evil one.
—Matthew 6:9-13

Our study of the Lord's Prayer includes prayers with fill-in-the-blanks and spaces for responding to God. Be honest with how you are thinking or feeling, with your questions, and with your hopes. Write them down and, when you finish the study, look back. You will see how God transformed and renewed your mind and heart.

Pray and allow time to respond:
Holy God, I, too, want to disentangle from all the things of the world and the thoughts going through my mind that keep me from living in peace and from the fullness of life you offer.
Right now that possibility seems _____
*to me because*_____
_____ .

I have opened this study guide. I've begun. It might not be a work project that will keep me from pursuing you, but it may be (ask God to show you what may keep you from spending time with him)_____
_____ .

Help me guard my time with you, God. I don't want to hope there will be time. I want to know when this study is to fit into my day. Just as I always take time for (something you do every day) _____ ,
when would you like me to spend time with you? _____ .

As the gardener said to Taylor, "You are in the right place," what does God say to you? Wait, listen, and write down what comes to mind.

Pray the Lord's Prayer, and end with praise to God.

WEEK ONE
DAY TWO
Settling into a chair under the maple tree's canopy of shade, my mind began to explode with questions: *What is this place, and why is it here? What is all that old stuff I saw on my walk? Why is this random gardener, Josh, taking such an interest in me? How could some ancient prayer I've recited all my life have the answers to the problems I've had most of my life?*

"Hey Taylor," Josh called. "Let me show you your room."

We walked up the flagstone walkway to the impressive mansion doors. Hand-carved mahogany trim framed the beveled glass windows.

> *...the words "how awesome is my God" resounded inside me, and I opened my mouth to say something to Josh.*

Through the clear panes I caught a glimpse of the rich red and brown patterned rug in the entryway.

The fragrance of the mountain air seemed to follow us inside; and I stayed right behind Josh as he went up the wide staircase.

The hallway rugs tucked the sound of our footsteps into the deep wool yarns, and the only thing I heard was a soft whirring as I passed by a closed door.

As we rounded a corner of the hallway, Josh opened a door to a room and said, "This one is yours." A stone fireplace, a four-poster bed with a down comforter, and a vase of wildflowers on the dresser greeted me. A spectacular view of the mountains drew me to the balcony's french doors.

Setting my bag down, Josh opened the glass doors, and we stood in silence at the balcony railing. I gazed at the majestic pine trees, the stream flowing through the valley, and the mountains in the distance. Suddenly, out of nowhere, the words "how awesome is my God" resounded inside me, and I opened my mouth to say something to Josh. He caught my eye.

"Taylor, it's from your heavenly Father—for you."

I couldn't quite take that in and was jarred from awe to reality. "That's an amazing gift from a father."

Josh glanced at me and then sat in one of the wicker chairs on the balcony. He gestured for me to do the same. The sound of the stream and intermittent calling of the finches quieted my thoughts.

Looking out over the valley, Josh asked, "Have you ever thought about the similarities between the way you've related to your earthly father and to God?"

"Not really." That idea had not even crossed my mind.

"Are you willing to take a look? As far-out as it may seem, it has to do with living in peace."

"Sounds a little random to me, but I am here to learn. Go ahead."

"Taylor, what is your dad like?"

"Oh, he's a great man. He's a dentist. He now works in his office a few days a week and volunteers in the free clinic a couple of days. When I was growing up, he was always leading medical mission trips. I went with him once."

"Did you enjoy that?"

"Sure. I guess I felt important because everyone practically worshipped him. He was the imported medical magician who could help everybody."

"What else did you do together?"

"He had me start piano lessons when I was five. His dream was for me to accompany him, and we'd play at receptions and banquets—you know, the child musician thing. He plays the sax, loves jazz. I never was any good at jazz piano; I don't have the improv knack. Just one of the ways he was disappointed in me, I guess."

"Hmmm, that's tough."

"Oh, but he was a good father. We always had what we needed. We got to go on family vacations, and it seemed as if he really liked being with us then. He taught me to fly kites, dig clams, and play cribbage. I was really very fortunate."

"Was he around home much when you were growing up?"

"My mom said he really wasn't a 'little kid' person. I remember him having dinner with us, but then he'd usually have ensemble practice or a mission meeting, or he'd need to catch up on paperwork from the office. I guess when he was home, the only time he seemed to notice me was when I was practicing the piano. Since I couldn't master it, that wasn't

16

always positive."

"So he wanted you to play the piano and it wasn't your passion. You mentioned there were other ways he was disappointed in you."

"I just don't think he ever got over the fact that I wasn't interested in what he was interested in, music and medicine. I was quieter—liked to draw and help with designing and building sets for plays. He never came to see what I'd done. He always told me he hoped I'd be a dentist or a physician's assistant so I could go on mission trips with him."

Josh looked reflective and a picture of my grandmother flashed through my mind. She would often pause as she considered what I'd said, just as Josh did.

"As you got older, what would you have liked from him?"

"I don't know. Lots more than I got." The answer was out there before I knew what I was saying. For some reason I felt embarrassed. I looked away from Josh's face and stared at my shoe, as though the pattern of my shoelaces would help me cope with disappointment I didn't really understand. I thought of my father's face—the comforting scruffy beard, the expectant look his sharp blue eyes would give me when he came back from work, as though asking if I'd made anything worthwhile of myself in the last ten hours.

> *I wanted to ask him questions about life, but I was afraid my lack of confidence would be another reason for him to be disappointed in me.*

"Lots more? What do you mean?" Josh's question interrupted my thoughts.

"Well, I guess I just wanted to know he thought I was okay—that I... mattered. I'd hear him on the phone with people, listening to them and encouraging them. He seemed to have a lot of compassion and wisdom for everyone else." I hadn't even realized I'd felt that way, and paused to take in what I'd said. Soon I continued, "I wanted to ask him questions about life, but I was afraid my lack of confidence would be another reason for him to be disappointed in me."

"That's hard—feeling like your father doesn't really understand you."

"Yeah." It felt good to have someone acknowledge that. I swallowed. "It was better to stay a little bit invisible. I guess I wanted him to be one of those dads who, you know, would put his arm around my shoulder and

17

say, 'Let's go get a Coke and talk about how to do life.' Yeah. That would have meant a lot."

Josh looked straight at me, "We all want to be known, don't we? And we want to know the way. It's a big and often confusing world. Taylor, you said your dad's name is Josh. When I told you my name was Josh, what went through your mind?"

"Hmm." I shifted in my chair, then blurted out, "I thought you really wouldn't be interested in me after you got to know me. Wow—I thought I'd end up disappointing you."

Josh smiled at me, put his hand on my arm, and asked, "Do you ever think God's disappointed in you—that he'll be there for others, but not for you?"

Nodding my head, the truth sank in. "Yes—actually, most of the time."

"Does your thinking line up with what you see in the Bible?"

I'd never been around anyone who asked questions like this. *What happened to just talking about the weather for awhile?* But at the same time, I realized I was excited to see what I'd discover.

"Probably not," I responded when I'd sorted some of this out. "But, I remember there's a psalm that says, 'Though my father and mother forsake me, the Lord will receive me.' Maybe I don't really believe that. I mean, I know the verse, and I guess it's true."

"So intellectually you know the truth about Father God. But if you were to think of him sitting down with you as I am, you probably wouldn't be comfortable? You wouldn't be sure if he approved of you or that you could be real with him? You'd have to try real hard to earn his favor?"

Do you ever think God's disappointed in you—that he'll be there for others, but not for you?

"Something like that. And I think I'm like that when I pray. 'Am I praying right? Am I remembering everything? Have I thanked God enough?' And then my mind wanders, and I get bored praying. I end up feeling guilty for being bored while I'm praying!"

Josh laughed knowingly, and then straightened his face. His laughter was a relief, but I was hanging on every word.

"Taylor, all of us have wounds we received as children; and as a result, lies we believe about ourselves and God. But there's good news: God can

18

rewrite our emotional history by bringing his truth into it and healing the ways our hearts have been hurt. He wants to remove the lies that keep us from knowing him as a loving, protective, and personally involved Father.

God can rewrite our emotional history by bringing his truth into it...

"It takes being honest with ourselves, repenting, forgiving, and receiving God's truth. Why don't you grab your Bible, go outside, and find a spot to sit and visit with God? I'll get a sack lunch from the kitchen and a workbook you can use for journaling and study. In a couple of hours, I'll meet up with you again."

A couple of hours? Visit with God? What is Josh thinking? I looked at him questioningly, but he was already headed toward the kitchen.

I'd never heard anyone be so perky about words like *repent* and *forgive*. *Well, maybe it won't be so bad.* A sigh snuck out of me as I went inside to grab my stuff. My room was filled with sunlight and the pine trees seemed to sparkle outside the window. I grinned to myself: *At least I can get some tanning in while I'm at this.*

REFLECT

1. In which ways do you identify with Taylor?

2. What was/is your father like?

3. How do you think your father saw you as a child and teen? Check all that apply and add your own:

☐ delightful   ☐ a problem   ☐ a wonder   ☐ annoying

☐ a joy   ☐ a burden   ☐ a friend   ☐ not worth his time

☐ a gift   ☐   ☐   ☐

4. Ask God to show you if there are any negative characteristics of your father or any ways he saw you that you are attributing to Father God.

5. **Read 2 Corinthians 10:5.** Write it as a prayer, and give God permission to change your way of thinking in any place where your beliefs do not line up with the Bible.

WEEK ONE
DAY THREE   REFLECT

Our relationships with our fathers affect us deeply. Whether or not our fathers are still living, our memories and past experiences with them continue to influence our lives. Often, other father figures become part of our life journeys, and they, too, can have a profound impact.

We are looking at our relationships with our earthly fathers not to be critical of the way we were raised, but to be set free from unmet expectations, judgments, and disappointments we have had. This freedom will enable us to love our parents more fully and will help lead us to a closer relationship with Father God. Be real. This is between you and God.

1. **Pray:** *Jesus, lead me in prayer. I give the Holy Spirit permission to search the deep recesses of my heart (see Psalm 139:23-24) in order to bring to light any places in my spirit where intimacy with Father God is blocked because of my relationship with my father. I'm willing to set my father(s) free from my judgments. Bring to mind anything I needed as a child but did not receive from my father or any words or actions that hurt me. Amen.*

2. Wait and listen to the Lord and also refer back to Day 2. Write down anything the Lord brings to mind that needs to be forgiven.

3. **Read Matthew 7:1-2.** Write it out.

We often make judgments against people, yet are unaware we have broken one of God's laws. In Matthew 7:1-2, we are warned not to judge others, or we will be judged in the same way.

One way we judge unknowingly is by making inner vows. For example, vowing "I will never be like my father" is a way of placing judgment upon your father for his behavior. Often the consequence of this judgment is that we carry on the behavior we disliked (or marry someone who exhibits it), and the cycle continues. It is only God's place to judge another person.

4. Pray out loud:

a) *I forgive my earthly father for* (Be specific. For example: for being cold and distant, for not giving me a sense of who I am, for not making me feel important):

b) *Forgive me, Lord, for judgments I have held against him and for vows I have made.* (Be specific.) *Set me free from them. I set my father free.*

c) *By the power of the shed blood of Christ, I break the lie that Father God will treat me in a negative way. I realize that lie is from Satan, and I will not cooperate with it.*

d) *Father God, what is the truth about you and my relationship with you?* Write it down.

e) *Father God, how do you see my earthly father?* Wait and see what comes to mind.

f) Pray a blessing over your earthly father, and thank God for the good you received from him. Write down your prayer. Thank God, also, for setting your father/Father relationships in order.

WEEK ONE
DAY FOUR   REFLECT

1. **Read Luke 15:11-24**, the Parable of the Merciful Father.
   a) From this parable, what similarities do you see in how God has treated you? Write them down.

   b) Write down verse 21 and read the definition of repentance.

   Repent: to change one's mind *(Strong's Concordance)*. In theology, to sorrow or be pained for sin, as a violation of God's holy law, a dishonor to his character and government, and the foulest ingratitude to a Being of infinite benevolence *(Webster)*.

   c) Ask God to show you why the son said he had sinned against heaven and his father. Write down what comes to mind.

In this parable, the son realized his foolishness and how he had not appreciated what he had in his father's house. He was convicted of his sin and knew he didn't deserve anything from his father. He shows us what repentance looks like.

Repentance is not simply feeling badly about something; rather, it is hating what we did or did not do. It is turning our backs on the sin and the power of Satan and walking in a new direction. It is admitting our wrongdoing, asking for forgiveness, and resolving to submit to God's better ways—not some time in the future, but now. This brings light into darkness and gives God permission to bring healing.

2. **KINGDOM LAB**—Have you ever had a sense of being unworthy or being a disappointment to God? Place yourself in the Luke 15 parable as the younger son. Repent of any ways you have wandered from God. Read Luke 15:22, and then in prayer, allow Father God to place the robe, ring, and sandals on you...

> **Best robe**: the father's own robe, replacing the dirt and rags of his son.
> **Ring:** the family ring signifying relationship and the authority of the father.
> **Sandals:** shoes worn only by sons, not servants, indicating a restoration of sonship and destiny.

...and then go to the banquet with him. He is celebrating over you! Write down what you experience.

WEEK ONE
DAY FIVE   REFLECT

Jesus begins the Lord's Prayer with "Our Father."

1. **Read John 20:17**. What is the significance of the opening words of Jesus' prayer?

Jesus introduces the Lord's Prayer through relationship. Throughout the Bible, relationship is very important to God. Think of the lists of genealogies. Perhaps you have often skimmed over them, wondering why they are there. Most of the genealogies go back many generations and are taken from the father's bloodline. A person's identity was directly related to whom his or her father was.

In John 20:17, it's as if Jesus says to his followers, "You may call God your Father. He's my Father and he's your Father—he's our Father. Who you are is directly related to who he is. And when you pray, address him as *Father*—think of him in this way."

2. **Read Romans 8:12-21**.

a) As a child of God, what are you promised?

b) In prayer, thank God for these amazing gifts and privileges.

3. **KINGDOM LAB**—The Aramaic word for *Father* is "Abba." Ask God how he would like you to address him in prayer. Ask him why he chose that term for you. Respond to him in a written prayer.

> *For you did not receive a spirit that makes you a slave*
> *again to fear, but you received the Spirit of sonship.*
> *And by him we cry, "Abba, Father."*
> —Romans 8:15

WEEK TWO
Heaven & Honor

The sound of footsteps on the pine needle-covered path caused me to look at my watch. It had actually been over two hours since I'd found the log picnic table in the midst of giant evergreens. The shade was welcome as I ate my lunch and went through the study Josh had given me.

"I thought I might have seen you awhile ago, wandering around checking the time," Josh kidded as he approached the table and sat down. "You look refreshed. How'd it go?"

Grinning, I stretched and shifted from the bench to sit on the table. "I sure was carrying around a lot of baggage from my dad." My own words caused me to pause, as if they were resonating within me. "I guess realizing that allowed me to look God in the eye for the first time in quite awhile."

"What did God show you?"

"I think my dad treated me like his father treated him. I realized he believes he has to earn God's favor. As a matter of fact, I felt sorry for him instead of hurt. I felt like praying for him."

Josh nodded knowingly, and I wondered if he might have been through the same thing. Then he commented, "You know, your willingness to bless your dad and, as a result, be healed yourself will break that generational pattern. When you have children, I believe they'll know they are unconditionally loved, and you'll be free to help them develop the unique gifts God will plant in them."

"I hope so. That's what I want. One more amazing thing happened just a few minutes ago. You know where it says to ask God how he would like us to address him in prayer?"

Josh nodded.

"I thought of the word *Daddy*, but that's what I called my dad when I was a kid, so that didn't seem big enough. I know some people pray to *Abba*, but all I could think of was the band and the songs in *Mama Mia! Father* is too formal for me. And then the word *Pater* came to mind. I think it means 'father' in some other language. But as soon as I thought of that word, I got choked up and just started crying—whatever that's about."

> *It seems as if my heavenly Father is a lot closer than heaven.*

Once again Josh looked at me and nodded. "*Pater* is 'father' in Greek. And those tears are probably a physical sign of the Holy Spirit touching your heart and making the Father's love and truth real to you."

Josh seemed to study my expression, as if checking to see if this was making sense. I wondered if the "Wow!" I felt showed on my face.

"Taylor, I think God is speaking loud and clear to you."

"Actually, it was a still, small whisper. But I think it is impacting me like thunder. It seems as if my heavenly Father is a lot closer than heaven." I paused and glanced up at the trees, not wanting this moment to pass too quickly. "Even now…it's like God is right here."

"Hmm. Sounds as if your idea of heaven could use some updating," Josh said, almost to himself.

The sparkle in Josh's eyes gave me a heads-up that he had a new plan, and I was right. He stood up, looked at me, and announced, "I just finished transplanting some raspberry bushes and could use a swim. Did you bring a swimsuit?"

It was my turn to nod.

"I'll meet you by the back door, and we'll continue our discussion down at the swimming hole."

"Swimming hole?" I grinned. "That sounds like heaven! I'll be right there."

REFLECT

1. What gives you the right to call God "Our Father"?

2. **Read John 14:6.** If you have never asked God for forgiveness of your sins, thanked him for sending his son Jesus to be your Savior, or committed your life to him as Lord—or if you've strayed from your commitment to him—let today be the day you have assurance that Father God is your Father.

a) Romans 10:9-10 says, "If you confess with your mouth, 'Jesus is Lord,' and believe in your heart that God raised Him from the dead, you will be saved. For it is with your heart that you believe and are justified, and it is with your mouth that you confess and are saved."

b) If you have questions about what this means, ask a pastor, Bible study leader, or Christian friend.

c) **Pray**:
God who saves, thank you that you are the way and the truth and the abundant life (John 14:6). *Thank you that you made a way for me to be in relationship with you through Jesus' death on the cross and his resurrection.*
Forgive me for all my sins: the things I've done that go against your ways, and the things I've left undone. Specifically, these sins stand out:

Thank you that Jesus paid my debt on the cross and that you have forgiven my sins. I admit there is nothing I can do to earn my salvation. I receive it as a gift of your mercy and grace (Ephesians 2:8,9).
I confess that Jesus is my Lord. Thank you for giving me new life through the Holy Spirit (Titus 3:4-7) *and that I am an heir, a son/daughter of God.*

d) Write out a prayer of gratefulness to God:

3. Be honest. What comes to your mind when you think of the word *heaven*? Write it down.

WEEK TWO
DAY TWO

With a Tarzan-like yell, Josh took a running swing from a thick rope tied to a high elm branch and landed in the middle of the swimming hole.

I, on the other hand, chose to test the cool water and then reluctantly plunged in, joining Josh as he tread water and sang some crazy song about jumping fish and dragonflies. *"Jumpin', jumpin', jumpin' fish— think yur about to git yur wish. Dive down real low, then up real high—yur gonna git that dragonfly!"* There didn't seem to be much of a tune, but with each *jumpin'* there was a lot of

> *The spiritual realm may be invisible to our eyes, but it's real.*

bobbing and splashing—followed by a twirl and clap that would have scared any dragonfly away.

"C'mon," Josh said, "Get your jumpin' fins on. We've got some dragonflies to catch!" *How long has it been since I've splashed around in a pool?* It was freeing, like being a kid again.

In high school, I'd had a youth group leader like that. Once we were painting a high cinderblock fence at the mission; it must have been 90 degrees out. Just when we were sure we were going to collapse before we were done, our leader called us over to a grassy area, gave us shaving cream beards, and handed us each a squirt gun. After a few minutes, he blew his whistle; those of us who'd lost most of our beards had to kneel down with our hands in the air. I still remember it was Cody who ended up with the most beard left. His picture was taken with us surrendering to him, singing "You are the Champion," right before our leader dumped a bucket of cold water on Cody's head. Ice cream bars cooled the rest of us off before we finished the project. *Maybe that's who Josh reminds me of.*

Coming up from underwater, wide-eyed Josh whispered, "Taylor, look below—quickly!"

Before I could ask, "Why?" his nose was plugged and his head down. Taking a big gulp of air, I joined him and dipped my head beneath the surface, opening my eyes underwater. Josh was pointing to my right at a school of fish coming out of the shadows of the rocks. They glimmered in shades of blue and green, and the sunlight seemed to deposit specks of glitter in the pool. I found myself floating on my stomach, not wanting any stray fish nibbling at my toes.

Swimming to shore, Josh commented, "It's a whole other realm down there, isn't it? Life is happening, and we're oblivious to it unless we *stick our noses into other fishes' business.*"

I rolled my eyes as Josh tossed me a towel and set up some canvas beach chairs. "So Taylor, there we were, floating around, and yet unaware there was more going on underwater than our legs moving to keep us afloat. What if we'd been swimming in a tropical reef? Think of what we would have seen when we looked beneath the surface!"

"Yeah, when I saw those beautiful fish I wondered what else in my life is close by that I am totally missing."

"Heaven's as close as your hand."

Now Josh was talking in riddles, I was sure, and I gave him my "I don't get it" look.

"Taylor, we are both physical and spiritual people. Our physical bodies live in the natural or physical realm and our spirits are a part of the supernatural or spiritual realm. You know those nesting dolls? It's as if the physical realm is nested inside the spiritual realm, yet they aren't separate. They interact all the time.

"Just because you couldn't see the fish when you were above the water didn't mean they weren't there. The spiritual realm may be invisible to our eyes, but it's real. God the Father, Jesus, the Holy Spirit, angels, Satan and his demons, and our human spirits make up the spiritual realm. Interaction is through prayer, blessings and curses, sin, righteousness, dreams and visions."

31

"Slow down! I thought I was over my head in that swimming hole, but this is really the deep end." Josh chuckled appreciatively, and I asked, "No, but seriously, how does that tie into heaven being as close as my hand?"

Josh pulled out a Bible and handed it to me. "Here, look up these verses and see what you find. Some beavers have been doing a little work I need to go and undo. Actually, I think God wants to undo some of your thinking—breakthrough a dam of tradition, so truth can flow in."

"Okay, okay. I'll be the eager-beaver for truth."

"You go, Bucky," Josh teased as he left me by the water.

REFLECT

1. **Write out:**
   a) **Genesis 1:1** *In the beginning... God created heavens & earth*
   b) **Genesis 1:27** *God created man in his own image*

   c) **Matthew 3:1,2** (the Greek word *eggizo* is translated "near" in NIV and "at hand" in NKJ)
   Repent for the kingdom of God is near
   d) **John 14:15-17**

As these verses show, we are both physical and spiritual beings. We sometimes long for more than we see on this earth. (**DIG DEEPER with Hebrews 11:13-16.**) At some level, most people recognize that this physical life is not the only reality and usually question, "What happens after I die?"

> **Heaven:** the abode of God; happiness, power, eternity *(Strong)*; place of renewal and perfection where no sin dwells and where there are resources to meet our physical, emotional, and spiritual needs.

2. **Read 2 Corinthians 4:16-18.** What perspective does this give you about life? Respond in prayer.

WEEK TWO
DAY THREE   REFLECT

1. The spiritual realm is invisible, but real. What are some things that are invisible but real in the natural realm (for example: radio waves)?

2. **Read Ephesians 6:10-12.**
   a) Do you ever sense a spiritual battle going on inside you? In what ways? Be specific.

   b) Where do you see signs of spiritual battles going on in the lives of family and friends and in our world?

3. **Read Ephesians 6:13-18 and 2 Timothy 1:7.** As believers, what is available to us in the spiritual realm? How might these spiritual tools affect the the way we live?

Why did Jesus think it was important for us to know about the spiritual realm and where the Father is when we pray to him? Why did he teach us to pray, "Our Father in heaven"?

After all, is there anything we truly need that is not available in heaven?

Perhaps it is because, when we understand that our Father dwells in the place of eternal and unlimited provision, we will not be hesitant to ask for what we need. After all, is there anything we truly need that is not available in heaven?

33

4. **Pray**:

Spirit of God, you are as close as my hand. You are within me. Forgive me for often living as if you are a distant God and as if my world is just about what I can see. Give me a passion for prayer, for blessing others, and for following your ways. I want to be a soldier in your spiritual army. I want my days on earth to make a difference for eternity, and I desire to cooperate with you. Is there any way I am enabling the evil one and his cause?

Listen and write what you sense.

Forgive me, Lord. What does it look like to cooperate with you?

From your spiritual storehouse, what do you have for me today?

Lord, give me eyes to see beneath the surface. I choose obedience, and I put on your army's uniform of love, Holy Spirit power, and self-discipline. In Jesus' name. Amen.

How do we respond to the provision of heaven and the love of our Heavenly Father being available to us? By praying, "Hallowed be your name."

WEEK TWO
DAY FOUR
I smiled as I held my hand out in front of me and thought of the saying, "talk to the hand." It reminded me of some of my junior high friends.

Josh came around the corner, "That's a lot to get your mind around, isn't it? 'The kingdom of heaven is at hand.'"

"When God seems far away, Josh, I think I'll just hold out my palm and remember he's right here, he's within me, he hears my whispers. Pretty amazing."

"How is it *amazing?*"

"Well, it's big. I mean really big. Like this thing I learned in Sunday School as a kid, but it never meant much to me: The Three O's."

"The Three O's?" Josh wondered.

"Omnipresent, omnipotent, omniscient. Those words used to make God seem kind of odd and distant; but now—I'm amazed—I think he's all of those things for me personally. God's really with me, he can take care of everything that concerns me, and he knows me—really knows me."

"How does that make you feel?"

"Free." I let out a long breath. "Like I'm beginning to hand over my responsibilities and worries to the One who can deal with them. I am tired of trying to understand —and fix—everything!"

"I sense you're grasping what *hallowed* means in the Lord's Prayer," said Josh. "When we pray, 'Our Father in heaven, hallowed be your name,' it's as if we're saying, 'May your name or all that you are be honored. Reveal your heavenly character in this world and in my life that everyone might see you clearly and be drawn to you.'"

> *Praise changes us.*
> *It helps us see God more clearly*
> *for who he really is.*

"You're right. God's revealing that to me, and I'm beginning to see who he really is. As it sinks in, I realize I can trust him more and want to truly live for him.

"But I've wondered about those words, *hallowed be your name.* Sometimes I've thought it strange that God wants people to go around praising him and telling him how great he is."

"Sounds as if you're beginning to see God knows we need reminders of who he is. Praise changes us," Josh explained. "It helps us see God more clearly for who he really is.

"Just as God doesn't want anyone to perish eternally (2 Peter 3:9), he also wants to provide for us, protect us, and love us. Think of a pair of eyeglasses. If God is seen and known through clear glasses, not ones clouded over by the world's misperceptions, men and women will flock to him. Don't you want to be a part of that adventure?"

"Uh, Josh—I think I'd like to make up for lost time. Do you have some Scriptures that would help me take the cloudiness off my 'what's God really like' glasses?"

"They're tucked in the back of the Bible. Take your time."

Then Josh pulled a felt pen out of his shirt pocket, took my hand, and wrote on my palm: *I love you—God.* "Just in case you decide to talk to your hand," he grinned.

REFLECT

1. When you remind yourself who God is, how does it affect you?

2. Could you identify with any of Taylor's misconceptions about speaking praise to God?

The Greek for *hallowed* is "to make holy, purify, or consecrate." *Hallowed be your name* can be translated, "May your name (character, reputation) be holy (revered, sacred, set apart)." It's as if we are praying, "Father, make your name holy to me and in all the earth. It is up to you. Help me grasp what that means. I'm available, but powerless without you."

Jesus is teaching us a kingdom principle: he invites us to pray and ask God and then leave our prayer with him while continuing to wait, watch, and act on his promptings.

3. Write out a prayer based on **Psalm 8** asking God to make his name hallowed. Then be specific. What places in your life do you want his character to be revealed? **DIG DEEPER with Psalm 113:1-3.**

WEEK TWO   REFLECT
DAY FIVE

1. **Read Luke 6:45.** Is the name of God holy and honored in your heart? Do you fill your heart and mind with things that focus on God and his character; or things that bring envy, lust, discontentment, or darkness? Ask God to reveal truth.

2. Job questioned God's ways and God answered him in Job 38-41. **Read Job 38:1-13** and then Job's reply in **Job 42:1-6. DIG DEEPER with Job chapters 38-41.**

   a) What stands out to you?

   b) Ask God to highlight one Scripture and reveal more to you through it. Wait and listen.

3. **KINGDOM LAB**
   Pray:
   Heavenly Father, the One close at hand: like Job, I know you can do all things, and no plan of yours can be stopped. So often I question your ways and what I see. Forgive me for forgetting who you really are.
   God, remind me how you revealed your character to me yesterday. (Wait and listen. Write down what comes to mind.)

What do you want me to remember about you today?

Lord, I'm willing to have your name be holy and honored in my heart. Cause me to turn from those things that elevate the evil one. Give me an obedient heart. Make every thought honor you and be life-giving to others and to myself. Strengthen me to hold fast to truth.

Pray "hallowed be your name" or **"holy be your name"** over and over. You may want to sing it. Let the Lord use the words and meditation of your heart to draw you to his perspective and heaven's way of seeing and thinking. Let him erase false images and rewrite God's truth upon the subconscious level of your heart.

> *The name of the Lord is a strong tower;*
> *the righteous run to it and are safe.*
> —Proverbs 18:10

4. Write down how God used your Kingdom Lab time.

WEEK THREE
Your Kingdom Come

WEEK THREE
DAY ONE "Dinner turned out a lot better than I expected," I remarked to Josh as we strolled through the estate in the evening.

"In what way?" he asked.

"When you told me trout was on the menu, I thought, 'Why didn't I bring something extra to snack on? I sure wasn't planning ahead—trout is usually pretty bony, and fishy.'

"Then you mentioned zucchini casserole, and I groaned inwardly; the only way I've ever liked zucchini is disguised in zucchini bread."

Josh grinned. "So how did you manage to clean your plate? There were no dogs under the table."

"Actually, it was all delicious. How'd the chef do it? The trout tasted..." I closed my eyes and savored the buttery-rosemary aftertaste in my mouth. "...well, it was fit for a king. And the cheeses and seasonings in the casserole gave me new respect for zucchini. I've had a total misperception of that vegetable—and I'm sorry."

"If you would have brought your own food, would it have been as gourmet?" Josh questioned.

I laughed, "Are you kidding? It would have been peanut butter sandwiches and chips—something quick and easy."

"So not as delicious and not as healthy for you, either? Sounds as if it was a good choice to put your trust in our chef."

I was beginning to see that most of my experiences at The Father's House had another layer to them. "This doesn't tie in to the Lord's Prayer by any chance, does it?"

"You're catching on, Taylor. That prayer is about our lives and how we relate to God. In the Bible, the Lord's Prayer is tucked in the middle of the Sermon on the Mount. Jesus teaches his disciples how things look differently when God is the king. He's really turning their thinking upside down. No longer were they to live by human reasoning or tradition; they were to trust that God knew what was best for them in every situation and that he was the good Father.

> *God wants his kingdom to be revealed on earth as it is in heaven. On earth, Taylor—not just revealed someday in heaven.*

"Think about what the disciples would have missed if they hadn't been teachable and willing to trust Jesus! They wouldn't have been a part of feeding the five thousand, of being sent out to heal, or most importantly—of knowing Jesus intimately."

"Wow, I didn't realize that what was offered for dinner had anything to do with trusting God. How many times a day do I do what's easy and satisfies me for the moment? How often do I even think what God's ways might be?"

"God wants his kingdom to be revealed on earth as it is in heaven. On earth, Taylor—not just revealed someday in heaven. He wants us to live as he created us to live—today."

We were nearing what appeared to be a junkyard; it seemed out of place on this estate. "I walked by here this morning, Josh. What's going on? Everything else I've seen on the property is beautiful. This is an eyesore."

"Before this land was The Father's House, it was used by a construction company as a dump site. You probably recognize a few things from demolished buildings."

Piles of scrap metal lay next to broken concrete and twisted rebar.

40

Pillars, an old mantle, and window frames without glass looked as if they might have some stories to tell. Mounds of dusty earth sprouting tall yellowing weeds were interspersed with old pipes, thick boards, and stacks of rusty light fixtures.

Despite their ugliness, dumps had always had a strange appeal to me—and I didn't want to stop looking around. "Amidst all this mess, there are some fascinating things," I commented. "Are you going to do anything with them?"

"Actually, I'll show you what we're already doing. Come this way, but watch for nails." Josh guided me through a narrow opening I hadn't noticed—between an abandoned bulldozer and stacks of disintegrating sheetrock. The debris was piled higher than my head. We wound around mounds of used bricks and tiles and then walked by weathered support beams and assorted pipes.

I was so focused on watching my step through the rubble that, when we came to a clearing and I glanced up, I was startled by the breath-taking view. We seemed to be near the edge of the property, and I took a few more steps forward. Looking out over the ravine in front of me, I saw a meadow dotted with wildflowers that appeared to carpet the land. It was quite a contrast to what I'd just walked through! There was a tall arch up ahead; Josh motioned for me to go on.

Stopping at the archway, I saw that it was made of beautifully restored pieces of wood. Old iron doorknobs were the only decoration, and they seemed to offer an invitation to step through.

Near the ravine was a large cross, and the mountains in the background rose up behind it. As I got closer, I saw benches made of aged beams set on artfully arranged brick supports. Broken tiles in intricate patterns covered the edges of the benches, and I sat down on one.

The cross was a work of art. Studying it, I realized it was built from some of the thick boards that had been split and cut down—probably to be hauled more easily. The crossbeam was notched and attached to the vertical piece with a combination of oxidized copper and tarnished brass wire.

Josh sat down beside me and spoke reverently, "We're in the process of building an outdoor chapel. You saw a junkyard—an *eyesore* as you called it, right?"

I nodded.

41

"But do you see how that trash has been used to make something beautiful and useful—something to be enjoyed? That's the way it is with the circumstances in our lives and in the world. They may look like a mess, but then God comes and brings his kingdom reign. He restores a relationship; he sets someone free from an addiction or unforgiveness; or he causes a door to open for a new job or friendship.

"We won't keep all the debris you walked through. Some will find new purposes; some won't be useful to this project or maybe any project and will be taken to a landfill. It's a work in progress.

> *That's the way it is with the circumstances in our lives and in the world. They may look like a mess, but then God comes and brings his kingdom reign.*

"When God's kingdom comes in our lives, our gifts and talents will be used for kingdom purposes. We may be redirected or equipped in new ways. We won't need some of the baggage we've carried around, like anger, pride, and worry. And we can throw them away, into the spiritual landfill, so to speak.

"Just as you still recognize that archway as pieces of wood and the bench-supports as bricks, you'll recognize people, situations, or communities after the kingdom of God comes to them. But there will be something new and different about them, too. That renewal process continues every day."

As Josh was talking, I thought of how arrogant I had been to the waitress who brought me the wrong sandwich on my drive to The Father's House and how I had barely looked at the cashier as I paid my bill at the café. *Was that conceited mindset becoming more a part of me—as if I were better than those serving me?* I took a deep breath, trying to release that attitude up to God.

"Just one more question, Josh. Who's building this chapel?"

"Kingdom residents," he answered.

"You and your riddles. What do you mean?"

"If God is your king," Josh replied, "you are a kingdom resident—living in both the natural and spiritual realms. The kingdom of God is here in its completion, but it is also still being completed. God asks us to join him in ushering in his kingdom on earth.

"You used to design sets for plays? How would you like to bring new life to some of these pieces that were junked? Your work could bring joy to others who come this way in the future."

"I'd like that, Josh. I really don't know where I'd begin, but I think that's an okay place to be."

"Tomorrow's another day. I've got a few more pages for your workbook. Maybe you can do a couple before bed, and then have them finished before breakfast. Life as a kingdom resident is amazing, Taylor. I've got more to show you, so get some rest."

We started our walk back to The Father's House in silence. I had a lot to think about, and the beauty of the night sky seemed to fill me with a peacefulness I hadn't felt for quite awhile. Then it was as if reality hit, and I broke the solitude. "I didn't see a TV in my room, Josh. Where would I find one? I always fall asleep with the late news."

"Will you trust the Father on this one, Taylor? Open the windows and listen...rest...pray."

"Father thinks he knows best again? I guess I'll call it the *trout and zucchini principle.* If you see me with dark circles under my eyes in the morning, though, don't offer me hibiscus tea. I take my coffee black!" Nearing the path to my room, I gave Josh my "I'm not kidding" look, followed by a grateful smile.

"Good night, Josh—and thanks. It feels like a relief to know God's kingdom is for now, and not to have to be the one in control."

REFLECT

1. There's nothing wrong with a peanut butter and jelly sandwich sometimes; but ask God if there's any place in your life where he's offering you something better and you're saying, "I'm fine. I'll just stick with what's familiar and comfortable." God might want to speak to you regarding your walk with him, a relationship, your health, a financial decision, or perhaps a ministry opportunity. Listen and write down what you hear or sense.

2. **Read Matthew 13:44** and write it out.

Kingdom of God like a treasure in a field

Pray: *Thank You, God, that your kingdom is a treasure to me in these ways:*

John 16:33
Peace
These things I have spoken unto . . .
I'm Prayed for
John 17:

Forgive me for times when I think of your ways as a burden or when I'm afraid of what the cost will be of following you. I lay my concerns before you (for example: it will take too much time; what about my friends?):

— choices — clarity
— hard to see the black & white of it,

Help me realize every day the treasure I have in you, my King. May I be willing to spend my life for you, knowing that the treasure of abundant, eternal life has been freely given to me.

Today, may my joy in this treasure spill out into every decision I make and every interaction I have. May your kingdom come in my life. In Jesus' name, Amen.

from the Counselor → how to go forth in joy

WEEK THREE
DAY TWO   REFLECT

In the Lord's Prayer, the word *kingdom* is not necessarily referring to a particular place, but rather a realm, rule, and reign. Where God is the king, the kingdom of heaven (or kingdom of God) has come.

1. **Read Luke 17:20,21.**

   a) What do you think the Pharisees were expecting?

   kingdom of God is within you not a physical place

   b) What realm was Jesus talking about, and how can we see where the kingdom of God is today?

   where God's goodness is manifested,

When God came to earth as Jesus, the man, he brought the rule and reign of the kingdom of God. Through Jesus, the sick were healed, the demonized set free, and the broken-hearted given hope.

Yet this was not the new world order the Jewish people were expecting the long-awaited Messiah to bring. There was no government take-over or well-equipped army. There was no surge of political or economic

> *Rather than a political and military revolution, God spearheaded a massive spiritual upheaval by raising his Son from the dead, and placing his Spirit within all those who believe.*

power for the Jews. And then there was a death on a cross. *What kind of God would allow his Messiah to be crucified?*

No wonder the Jewish people were confused. Rather than a political and military revolution, God spearheaded a massive spiritual upheaval by raising his Son from the dead, and placing his Spirit within all those who believe. Now every Christ-follower has access to God's kingdom power.

When we as believers know the heart of God and understand the kingdom principles, we are able to cooperate with God's reign and be a part of bringing his kingdom to all situations. The kingdom of heaven is present and available to every person.

Through praying, "your kingdom come," and being submissive to God's ways, we participate in the spiritual upheaval of bringing heaven to earth.

2. Let today be the day you activate God's kingdom coming to places in your life.

Pray: *Our Father in heaven, hallowed be your name* (pause and remind yourself who God is; speak it back to him).

Your kingdom come on earth as it is in heaven in these specific places in my life (write them down):

May there be a spiritual upheaval in every life and situation I've lifted to you, Lord. May you reign as King. In Jesus' name, Amen.

WEEK THREE
DAY THREE

1. **Read Psalm 103** and write out verse 19 (this is both seen and unseen).

   a) What is revealed about God's character in this psalm?

b) From this psalm, what does the Lord ask of you?

c) Read the psalm again, asking God to highlight and personalize one specific thing about his kingdom rule and reign. Write it down, ask him to reveal more about it, and then respond to him in a written prayer.

> *Jesus said, "My kingdom is not of this world. If it were, my servants would fight to prevent my arrest by the Jews. But now my kingdom is from another place."*
> *"You are a king, then!" said Pilate.*
> *Jesus answered, "You are right in saying I am a king. In fact, for this reason I was born, and for this I came into the world, to testify to the truth. Everyone on the side of truth listens to me."*
> —John 18:36–38

- **Are you willing to live set apart from the values and traditions of this world and culture?**

- **Are you ready to be on the side of truth?**

- **Are you willing to let Jesus be your King?**

WEEK THREE
DAY FOUR   REFLECT

Remember the Lord's Prayer is found in the middle of the Sermon on the Mount, a teaching Jesus gave his followers. It begins in Matthew 5 and goes through chapter 7, giving examples of how things are when God is king.

Jesus was introducing a spiritual upheaval that would clash with the culture and with humanity's sinful nature; it would affect every thought, word, and action of his followers.

1. **Read Matthew 5:1-12**, the Beatitudes.

   a) These statements compare kingdom or eternal values with temporary or worldly values. They were in contrast to the way of thinking in Jesus' day. Do you see ways they conflict with our culture's present-day values and thinking? List several.

   b) **KINGDOM LAB:** Ask the Holy Spirit to point out a particular *blessed* (sense of well-being) that he wants to talk with you about. Listen. Write down what you sense the Lord is saying to you.

   (Example from Matthew 5:6: *Lord, I think you want to talk to me about hungering and thirsting for righteousness—for truth* (wait and listen). *Lately I seem to be dissatisfied with my family and their attitudes, with my job and with the little time I have to do what I want. It's as if my appetite for things to be different is insatiable. I realize my wants can be a bottomless pit. There's always "just one more thing"* (pause—listen). *Lord, your Word says you are the living water and the bread of life. May*

I fill up on your truth. May I know your ways. What does it mean to "be filled" (Matthew 5:6)? After listening, I think that knowing your truth will set me free from discontent. It will bring well-being to my soul and will permanently fill the empty places in my heart. My focus will not be on myself, but on your kingdom and eternal things.)

c) **Pray:** *God of blessing and well-being, may my worldly thought patterns, habits, and behaviors be conformed to the ways of your kingdom. May your kingdom come into this place in my life. I will act on the truths you showed me by:*

What is your promise to me today?

In Jesus' name, Amen.

> *"What shall we say the kingdom of God is like, or what parable shall we use to describe it? It is like a mustard seed, which is the smallest seed you plant in the ground. Yet when planted, it grows and becomes the largest of all garden plants, with such big branches that the birds of the air can perch in its shade."*
> —Jesus' words in Mark 4:30-32

WEEK THREE
DAY FIVE   REFLECT

KINGDOM LAB: Have you ever been in a time-management class and been instructed to write down how you spend every minute of your day? The purpose is to bring reality to the way your day is used and then to determine changes in order to be more efficient or productive.

Let's look not only at how we spend our time, but also at what we think about. Take a moment and write out a general overview of your day and what was going through your mind.

What I Did	My Thoughts
(general time blocks)	*(During this time, my thoughts were focused on* _____. *I also thought about* _____ .*)*

Do you see any places where you were operating as *king* and not submitting to God's *rule and reign*?

We want to give God an opportunity to point out places where we are being rebellious because those are areas he has something better in mind for us.

Ask the Holy Spirit to highlight one thought pattern that he would like you to address. Put a star (*) by it.

1. **Read Matthew 6:25-34.** Through these verses, what is God saying to you in relation to the Kingdom Lab results?

KINGDOM LAB, continued: For God's kingdom to come, we have to step down as king and allow him to reign. Be honest. How's it going with you as king in the area God pointed out? Do you have the wisdom, the resources, or the power to change the situation on your own?

Are you willing to pray the following?

Our Father, once again, I realize I've acted as if I think I can do a better job as king in this situation than you can. Forgive me for my foolishness and lack of trust in you. What is the truth, Lord? Listen and write it down.

In prayer, picture yourself sitting on the throne in this situation. How does it look with you in charge? Write it down.

Pray: *Lord Jesus, would you come now and sit on this throne? I want to place the crown on your head. I step down and allow you to reign.* Write down or draw your prayer experience.

> *For the Kingdom of God*
> *is not a matter of talk but of power.*
> —I Corinthians 4:20

Lord, I ask for your kingdom to come into the place you brought to mind. Set things right. Let these places be on earth as they are in heaven. Is anything in my thinking, attitudes, or actions blocking your kingdom from coming? Listen and write it down.

If something came to mind, ask for forgiveness and ask God how to think or act differently. Write down the insight God gives you.

King Jesus, thank you that your kingdom has come. Thank you that even though circumstances or relationships may look like a mess, an eyesore, or hopeless to me, you are a God of redemption. I believe you will work all things together for good because I trust you (from Romans 8:28). Give me a picture of promise or hope:

Thank you, reigning King. I worship you.

Now to the King eternal, immortal, invisible, the only God, be honor and glory for ever and ever.
Amen
—I Timothy 1:17

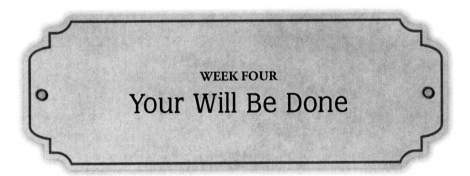

WEEK FOUR
Your Will Be Done

A knock on the door woke me from morning dreaminess and reminded me I wasn't at home. *What time is it, anyway?*

"Room service, Taylor. May I set your hibiscus tea inside the door?"

"Only if it smells and tastes like hot black coffee. Come on in, Josh."

I'd pulled the soft quilt up under my chin and was enjoying the luxury of feeling rested and still being in bed. Josh set a tray down on the table, and the aroma of coffee perked me up. "That's the best smelling hibiscus tea I've ever been around," I said with a grin.

"Breakfast will be on the sun porch in an hour. Come ready for a short hike." Josh glanced out the window, "It's a stellar morning out there."

Josh's cheerfulness was contagious, I realized as I took my coffee out on the balcony. The morning greeted me with a smile of sunlight and a hug of crisp mountain air. Standing at the railing, I took in the beauty and majesty. *Yes, Lord, you are King. There is no Creator on this earth other than you—no one else who can bring to life even a blade of grass or set one bird soaring in the sky.*

I decided to go back in for my Bible and turned to the psalm I'd studied last night. Feeling a little Shakespearian on my balcony, I set my coffee on the arm of the chair and read to the Lord and his creation:

55

Praise the Lord, O my soul;
all my inmost being praise his holy name.
Praise the Lord, O my soul, and forget not all his benefits...
The Lord has established his throne in heaven,
and his kingdom rules over all...
Praise the Lord, O my soul.
—From Psalm 103

Josh was sipping orange juice when I joined him at the table on the sun porch. "So—am I going to learn to like porridge and runny poached eggs this morning?" I asked as I pulled out my chair.

"If that hibiscus tea tasted okay to you, I think you'll be just fine." Josh's teasing and warm smile made me feel comfortable, and I looked forward to whatever the day held. He reminded me of my sixth grade teacher, who seemed to enjoy my unique way of looking at things. She had even encouraged me when I wanted to build an amusement park for the classroom hamsters. During that time, she called me 'Diz' and would sometimes let the 'Disney Studio Team' stay in from recess and work on our project. Looking back, I could now see that her joy in my creativity is one of the reasons I'm in a job I love. *I wonder how many people Josh has also helped set on the right course. Have I ever done that for anyone?*

> *As Josh blessed our meal and time together, I wondered why I assume God's plan for me is something I won't like, something difficult or dull...*

The scrambled eggs and blueberry pancakes that Josh brought to the table looked delicious. As Josh asked the blessing over our meal and time together, I wondered why I always assume God's plan for me is something I won't like, something difficult or dull...or even scary.

The herbs mixed in the eggs tasted fresh, and the blueberries were the sweetest I'd ever had. "Josh, as you were praying I realized I'd thought my room in The Father's House would be a bunk bed with a thin mattress, bare walls, and maybe a small window—that I'd be one of a crowd of people here, and breakfast would be something I wouldn't like. I know the Bible says God provides everything we need, but this seems to go beyond *daily* bread! It seems almost extravagant."

Josh smiled, "Well, just as your view of Father God was tied into your relationship with your earthly father, most likely your idea of God's will is tied into life circumstances you've misunderstood or hurtful things you've blamed on God."

Josh continued eating as I thought about that. "When you said the word *blame*, I realized I have held something against God. That sounds so arrogant on my part, though. I know God's ways are not to be questioned; they have purposes greater than I can understand."

"Taylor, he's big enough for your questions and for your doubts. Put them out there so he can deal with them."

I thought for a moment, and then began, "Well, it's been three years now, but a relationship with the person I was sure I was going to marry ended. I had my future planned out. We

> *Taylor, he's big enough for your questions and for your doubts. Put them out there so he can deal with them.*

dated for a year, and then—I don't know—it just all fell apart. I still don't understand why. I felt as if God didn't want me to be happy. I spent a year moping around about it, feeling angry, trying to forget it, throwing away old mementos and then regretting it—what a waste of time. Then I just stopped making an effort to heal from it and threw myself into my job so I'd have to concentrate on something else. I decided to try being the youngest person ever to make partnership in my company."

"What a big disappointment, Taylor. I'm sorry."

"Yeah. I guess I'm still not really over it."

"Must not seem to you as if God's will was *good, pleasing, and perfect* like Romans 12:2 talks about."

"Maybe for God, but not for me—at least not that I can see."

"What do you think you believed about God's character from that experience?" Josh asked.

As I drank the last of the fresh squeezed orange juice, I knew my beliefs didn't line up with what I was experiencing here. "I had thought God didn't want me to have any fun—that he wanted me to suffer. Maybe he wanted to teach me something, for my own good of course."

"Taylor, while you were dating, did the relationship draw you closer to God or farther away?"

God sees the big picture.

I thought for a moment and realized our dates pretty much took up every spare minute I had. "We enjoyed being together. On the weekends we went cross-country skiing, hiking, or boating with friends. We both believed in God, but it's something we never really talked about."

"From God's perspective, how do you think he saw your relationship?" Josh asked.

"Mm, he might have thought we were a little too focused on ourselves."

Josh raised an eyebrow. "Ourselves? What do you mean?"

"As the Father who enjoys spending time with me, he probably felt displaced—as if I'd put someone else where he belongs."

Josh nodded, giving me time to hear what I'd said. "I don't have the answers for you, but I do know the character of God and know he can be trusted. When we're confident in his character, we can believe he wants to bless us and pour his love out in extravagant ways.

Taylor, we can pray for God's kingdom to come all we want; but if we aren't willing to submit to his will if it looks different from our will, then we're standing in the way.

We can't always see God's plan, but he has one. God sees the big picture. We can trust him."

"I'd love to believe that."

"Taylor, we can pray for God's kingdom to come all we want; but if we aren't willing to submit to his will if it looks different from our will, then we're standing in the way.

"I think it might help you to look up these Bible verses while I get things ready for our hike. I'm hoping God will show you his *eggs and pancakes principle*." Josh winked, and I smirked back.

"Okay, okay—do you have a frying pan I can sit in? I think some of my thinking is about to be scrambled."

REFLECT

1. Like Taylor, do you ever dread or fear God's will for you, thinking it will be porridge and runny eggs rather than blueberry pancakes and scrambled eggs mixed with herbs? Ask God if any life circumstances have contributed to wrong beliefs about God's will. Write down what you think he's saying. If something specific comes to mind, ask God to show you where he was or is in those places.

After waiting awhile, if you can't see where God was or is in those places, read John 11:35. Does it apply?

2. **Read Romans 12:2.**

a) How does this verse describe God's will?

b) How are we to test and approve God's will? Practically speaking, how do we do that?

3. **Pray:** *Good and loving Father God, I realize my view of you and your will for me has been distorted by life circumstances. Forgive me for thinking* (look back at question one)*:*

What is the truth?

Even in those life circumstances where I can't see any purpose or your handprint, I want to trust that your will for me today is good, pleasing, and perfect. May I cooperate with you as you renew my mind. Transform me from the inside out. In Jesus' Name, Amen.

WEEK FOUR
DAY TWO   REFLECT

The word *will* in the Lord's Prayer is translated from the Greek, "the want of you." It's defined as "specific purpose, desire, choice, pleasure." When we pray, "your will be done," it's as if we are saying, "Father, may what you want or desire be done."

1. **Read Isaiah 46:8-13,** which was written to the Israelites, God's chosen people, when they were wavering between God and pagan gods.
   a) What does God want the Israelites to know about his will? What does he have for them?

   b) Ask God what he is saying to you through these verses. Write it down and respond to him. Note that the Greek word for *salvation* is "sozo," meaning "saved, healed, and delivered." It is an ongoing process in our lives.

2. **Read Ephesians 1:3-14.** What do you learn about God's will?

3. **Read Matthew 26:39-42.**
   a) What would have happened if Jesus had chosen comfort rather than obeying his Father's will?

   b) How might this have affected you?

   c) Spend a few minutes in prayer, thanking Jesus for his obedience to God's will and for how it has impacted your life.

WEEK FOUR
DAY THREE

REFLECT

In order to see the fullness of God's will, think of creation before sin entered the world. God wants us to live in that spiritual, emotional, and physical wholeness and well-being. Satan, however, wants to steal wholeness from us. We are often fooled by his tactics and become divided from God through our pride, our wrong perception ...our sin.

It is possible to have God's kingdom rule explode within our spirits, and to live more like Jesus lived—today.

The will of God is to destroy the works of the devil (1 John 3:8), so he sent Jesus (meaning "God saves") to restore his will—on earth as it is in heaven. Jesus came to bring the dwelling place of God—heaven—to the dwelling place of man—earth. Jesus brought the two realms together.

It *is* possible for us to live in the freedom and fullness Christ offers—not just after we die, but here on earth. It *is* possible to be restored to our right minds, to have God's kingdom rule explode within our spirits, and to live more like Jesus lived—today.

1. **Read Ephesians 5:15-18.**

    a) If we do not seek to understand God's will, what are we?

    b) God's will is that we be filled with the Spirit—with his very life—and with all the love, truth, and power Jesus had while he was on earth. We are made in God's image and have now been filled with his Spirit. We are meant to be an army of Christ-like warriors bringing God's love, truth, and power to the world. Have you enlisted? If not, will you today? Respond to God in prayer.

2. **Read Isaiah 61:1-6.** From these verses, how will the fullness of God's will be seen in us? Personalize your response:

a) *God's will is for me to:*

b) *I am able to do his will because:*

3. **Pray.** Ask God for one specific way he wants his will to be done in you or through you today. Wait, listen, talk with him about it. Then respond to him in a written prayer.

WEEK FOUR "Taylor! Watch out! Jump to your left!"

DAY FOUR I, too, heard the sudden rumbling from above and all I wanted to do was duck down on the trail and cover my head.

"Taylor! Now! Go left!"

Everything in me screamed, "*Duck!*" I wasn't sure what was beneath the bushes on my left, and it looked as if they might be on the edge of a rocky cliff.

"Go! Taylor, move!"

The noise above us grew louder. I fought my instinct and finally dove, eating airborne dirt and feeling the rocky ground hit my chest as rocks tumbled by me. Coughing, then catching my breath, I looked up from the thorny bushes that had stopped my fall. Dust clouds and a stunned Josh greeted me. "Are you okay?" Josh asked, rushing over to me.

"I didn't know cactus grew in this part of the country," I groaned as I got up, carefully trying to avoid any more thorns.

"That was a close one," Josh said, giving me a hand. "I've seen signs of rockslides before, but I've never been in one until now. The trail widens up ahead. We'll take a water break."

Josh and I sat on a log and I told him that, when I heard the rumbling, I had wanted to duck down and cover my head rather than do what he said.

"Yeah, then you would have been a *sitting duck*. Those rocks were perfectly lined up to hit you. I was far enough behind to have a clearer view of what was going on, Taylor. My perception was more accurate."

Pulling a tiny thorn out of my hand, I said, "Okay Josh. This is too much. How did you get those rocks to roll just at that moment so we'd have another analogy to the Lord's Prayer?"

"Nothing is wasted in the kingdom of God, Taylor," Josh chuckled. "What comes to mind?"

I turned to look back at the trail. "In my life, I so often think I know what's best, or at least what I want. But my instincts can be wrong or my perception limited. I know I let the culture speak to me rather than letting God speak. I watch the news and think I can determine the future. I turn to self-help books or talk shows for guidance rather than the Bible, not even considering that God might have something to say. I make decisions or form beliefs based on what's happening around me rather than asking him for the big picture, for his eternal plan. It's like I'm a sitting duck for Satan's landslide."

> *I let the culture speak to me rather than letting God speak.*

"For your safety, you had to submit to something you didn't understand, right, Taylor? You had to say to your flesh or your nature, 'No! Go left!'"

"There was a battle going on inside me," I agreed, reflecting on the past half hour. "I know it was just a few seconds, but I had quite an argument with myself."

"Just as I didn't want you taken out by rocks," Josh replied, "God's will is that your desires be his so that Satan can't steal from you—that he can't take you out by deception.

"There is often a time of fighting against our own will—against our

Just as I didn't want you taken out by rocks, God's will is that your desires be his so that Satan can't steal from you—that he can't take you out by deception.

laziness, our pride, the way we've always done things. As we continue to do this, we are remolded, and our desires become God's desires. His nature becomes our nature. Choosing God's way is worth the discipline. It brings us the peace, joy, and purpose we long for.

"Taylor, take last night. You asked about a TV. Did you miss having one?"

"I wasn't sure what to do with myself at first," I answered. "But then I turned out the lights and started thinking about the kingdom of God and its being on earth *now*. That idea filled me with hope and excitement for following God. I really slept peacefully."

"So, when you go to bed after watching the news, what is on your mind?" asked Josh.

"Good point. It sure could be a part of the anxiousness I often feel in the middle of the night. You told me to listen and pray. When I woke up last night, I thanked God for the stillness and the ways he has encouraged me—for bringing me here.

"But Josh, this place is unique. I don't have any other responsibilities, and you're here to teach me. At home, I have so much going on. I need TV."

"Taylor, I'm not saying you have to get rid of your TV, but do you think it cares about you more than God does? Has it crowded him out of your evening or given you no time for a thought of your own in the morning? Do you turn to it for companionship or to get relief from the cares of the world?

"If you want his kingdom to come and his will to be done in your house as it is in his house, you may need to make some changes."

If you want his kingdom to come and his will to be done in your house as it is in his house, you may need to make some changes.

"Josh, it all makes sense here. I think I can trust God, but I'm not sure I can trust myself. I've tried to make changes before, but I seem to always cave in."

We watched a full-cheeked squirrel dart up a tree and a bird make a nest overhead. *Consider how the lilies grow, consider the birds of the air that do not sow or reap...*

"It's not hopeless, Taylor. God's kingdom reign is internal. Allow him to transform your thinking, and you'll see external changes, too. Jesus brought the kingdom of God to earth. God's good purpose and pleasure can happen in your life, in your heart, in your house, Taylor."

"I'm beginning to really long for that. I think I've been missing out."

"On our way back, consider how you can know God's will and what might keep you from cooperating with it," Josh suggested.

"Okay, but you don't have any more rockslides planned, do you?" I gave Josh my "you'd better watch it" look.

"Don't worry, Taylor, just keep going. I'll give you plenty of warning so you'll avoid the man-eating crocodiles in the creek up ahead."

REFLECT

Like Taylor, we are sometimes unaware of what we really need. We get confused by the busyness of life, by our striving for comfort, and by the kingdoms we have built for ourselves. No matter how hard we try, we often can't figure out how to make life work.

In "Father, your will be done," Jesus is teaching us to humble ourselves, to admit we do not see the whole picture, and to ask God to make his will happen. We say, "God, you figure it out. I'm depending on you. Show me how to cooperate with you."

1. Is there a place in your life where you have prayed for God's kingdom to come, but it seems you are unwilling to step back or submit to God's way of working through things? Ask God, and write it down.

Perhaps you say, "I'd cooperate with God's will if I knew what it was." Be encouraged, there are ways to gain insight into his will, and we know his will always lines up with the Bible.

Discerning God's Will

1. Determine what you're thinking or wanting, and offer it back to God. Give it up. Lay down your own ideas for how things should work out or happen. Go to God with no agenda.

2. Ask God to speak to you through the Bible, either in your regular study, or by leading you to specific Scriptures.

3. Ask God to make his desires your desires and to change your heart or thinking if need be (...for it is God who works in you to will and to act according to his good purpose {Philippians 2:13}).

4. Wait (look watchfully with expectation). Pray. Listen. Be in God's Word. Be sure your desires line up with Scripture.

5. When you have direction, ask God for his timing. Wait and watch until you sense the Holy Spirit showing you it's time to act. Realize, for the time being, God may want your only action to be prayer.

2. Briefly summarize each step in your own words.

1.

2.

3.

4.

5.

3. **Read Psalm 37:3-9.**

a) From this psalm, how do we cooperate with God so his desires become our desires?

b) What steps for knowing God's will do you see in this psalm?

c) Ask God to highlight a verse and to talk with you about it. Write down what you hear, sense, or think, as well as your response to God.

4. Think of a place in your life where you are seeking God's will. Begin praying through the five steps of discerning God's will; listen to God's leading. Write down your prayer and come back to this page later to continue the process.

Delight yourself in the Lord
and he will give you the desires of your heart.
—Psalm 37:4

WEEK FOUR
DAY FIVE   REFLECT

In the Lord's Prayer, we are asking for God's kingdom ways to come to specific situations, and we are saying we're willing to cooperate with his will. As we pray "on earth as it is in heaven," it's as if we are saying, "God, you make it happen in our house as it is in your house."

Did you notice that the prayer is not what will be in heaven, but what is in heaven? It's about the present as well as the future.

Did you notice that the prayer is not what will be in heaven, but what *is* in heaven? It's about the present as well as the future.

Because Jesus submitted himself to the Father's will, it is now possible for God's will to be done today—in us. If we are willing to submit to the Father's will, who knows how many lives that decision may affect?

Let's look at a few more ways we can know God's will:

1. Read Matthew 6:33.

   a) We will be more able to know God's will if we:

   b) Ask God what that looks like for you, practically, today.

2. Read John 5:19-20. If Jesus was totally dependent on his Father to know how to live each day, we need to be too.

   a) Ask God to show you three things he is doing in your life or in the lives of those around you.

   1)

   2)

   3)

b) How do you know God is the one doing them?

If we are willing to submit to the Father's will, who knows how many lives that decision may affect?

3. KINGDOM LAB:

Pray: *Father God, thank you that you are at work around me. Please show me which of the things you brought to mind in question 2a) you would like to show me more about. I bind the voice of the enemy and my own self-talk. May your voice be the only voice I hear. In Jesus' name I pray, Amen.*

a) What would God like you to pray more about?

b) Ask God to show you his "as it is in heaven" perspective for this person or situation. Write it down.

c) **Read John 6:38-40.** Ask God for more insight through this Scripture. Write it down.

d) **Read I Thessalonians 5:16-18.** Apply this Scripture to what God has shown you. Thank God that his desire is for his kingdom to come, for his will to be done in this life and situation—as it is in heaven. Rejoice, pray, thank; rejoice, pray, thank. Write your prayer.

Give Us This Day

WEEK FIVE Sorting through the discarded items at the
DAY ONE construction dumpsite, I'd come across some real
treasures. An old coal bucket, some iron window
grates, and a broken pillar with intricately carved details spoke of
possibility to me. My imagination was in full gear, and I pulled some of
the pieces into the clearing.

Dusting off the mantle I'd seen yesterday, I envisioned it as part of a
Communion table for the chapel. Unfortunately, it was way too heavy for
me to dislodge from the pile. I had some good ideas but was beginning
to feel overwhelmed. *On my own, can I make much of a difference here? Is
this even worth it?*

The grates must have been for the bottom half of narrow windows. I
stood them on end and pushed the iron spikes into the earth. *Just the right
height.* Holding the coal bucket a few inches lower than the top of the
grates, I pictured a firebox for Ash Wednesday services. I also remembered
the campfire on the last night of church camp and how we wrote words
like *pride, sarcasm,* or *rebellion* on pieces of driftwood and tossed them in
the fire, symbolizing repentance and our intent to live free of those things
when we went home. Watching my piece of wood turn to ash reminded
me of God's willingness to set me free from guilt and shame and that he
no longer counted my sin against me. Perhaps my findings could be used

71

> *Watching my piece of wood turn to ashes reminded me of God's willingness to set me free from guilt and shame and that he no longer counted my sin against me.*

in that way, too.

"Let me guess—a very deep bird bath?" Josh asked. I shook my head *no*, and he tried again. "You're not planning on heaping burning coals on anyone's head, are you?"

Josh's arrival made me feel less overwhelmed. As I explained my ideas, I could see that he saw my vision. "The thing is, Josh, I feel stuck. I have the ideas, but I don't have the strength to lift the pieces on my own. I also don't have many carpenter skills. What good are design possibilities if I can't make them happen?"

With an understanding nod, Josh walked over to the grates and picked them up. "Grab the bucket, Taylor, and let's take these to the front of the chapel. Before my creativity will kick in, I think I'll need a rest on the benches. Digging rocks out of a new garden area has totally zapped me."

As we sat down, Josh took a minute to gaze at a flock of geese drafting in its "V" formation, probably migrating back for the summer. "Taylor, have you ever thought about why Jesus used the words *us* and *our* in the Lord's Prayer: 'Give *us* this day *our* daily bread'?"

"Um," I stammered, feeling dense. "Not really. Maybe because he knew we'd say it together in church."

> *What if you considered the us being everyone who calls God, 'Father'—that is, every Christ-follower in the world?*

"The disciples asked Jesus how to pray. He probably knew they would often pray on their own, yet he used corporate thinking in his answer. It does seem natural to pray that way when we're in a group, but by yourself, how do you relate to those words?"

How does Josh think of these questions? "Actually, I suppose it makes the prayer impersonal to me. Maybe if I thought of the *us* being my family and friends."

"What if you considered the *us* being everyone who calls God, 'Father'—that is, every Christ-follower in the world?"

"Whoa! I can't get my mind around that one. It's like asking how many pennies it would take to circle the globe. Just too big to think about."

"Okay, Taylor. Give God a chance to show you what he means. Be still and ask him in prayer."

Josh was quiet, as if he was waiting for something. "Sure, I'll do that sometime, Josh."

"Why not now, Taylor? I'll start you off. Father God..." he began. I bowed my head. Josh was seriously thinking God would explain this to me. "...thank you for the Holy Spirit who reveals truth to us, who helps us understand your Word and your heart. Show us why you ask us to pray using *us* and *our*. Please speak to Taylor's spirit through a thought or a picture. In Jesus' name."

In the quiet I thought, "I better figure this out." Nothing came to me as my mind went through possible ideas. A breeze blew across my face and with it the thought, "Be still." I breathed in the freshness of the air and breathed out my own ideas.

> *A breeze blew across my face and with it the thought, "Be still."*

I breathed in the truth that I have a good heavenly Father and then breathed out my fear that I wouldn't hear anything. I waited in the quiet of the afternoon.

The thought of the pennies circling the globe came to mind. But then the pennies were people—men, women, and children of every nationality, holding hands and praying in hundreds of languages, "Our Father in heaven...give us this day our daily bread." I was in that circle, holding hands with my global Christian sisters and brothers—part of a family praying for, as well as with, the ones in Cambodia, the ones in Mexico, the ones next door. And, they were praying for me. We were one in purpose and in need of our Father's provision and help.

Looking up at the cross, I told God how sorry I was for being so focused on myself—on what I wanted or felt I needed. Being the youngest partner in my company suddenly seemed to have lost its urgency. *What's my striving about? What am I hoping to gain?*

73

Telling Josh about my vision, he smiled. "That's a beautiful picture, Taylor. You're beginning to see how interconnected and interdependent we are in the kingdom of God. Do you know how unique your mental pictures and creativity are? Yet you seem concerned about not having the skills to bring them to life. There are others who have the talent and need someone to give them the vision or plans. In fact, there's a group of craftsmen here for a few days looking for projects. They've been organizing our workshop and setting up new equipment that was donated. Let's go meet them."

Why is it I often think God expects me to figure it out on my own?

As we walked, I reflected out loud, "In my job I'm part of a team, and I see how necessary and effective the team approach is. Why is it I often think God expects me to figure it out on my own?"

"Kick the coal bucket on that idea, Taylor. You're just one part of the body of Christ. Is there freedom in that thought?"

"Freedom from pride, I guess. Take me to some biceps and skilled hands. I've got an eye for creativity, but I could sure use some help."

REFLECT

1. Have you ever considered praying for the entire kingdom of God as you pray the Lord's Prayer? Why or why not?

2. **Read John 17:20-26.** Ask God to show you reasons he wants us to be united with all believers.

3. **Read Romans 12:3-8.**

a) Just as the physical body is under the command and authority of the brain, under whose command and authority is the body of Christ?

b) If you are a follower of Christ, then you are part of his body. Ask God to show you the gifts you have for the body. How are you using them?

c) Are you ever envious of gifts others have that are different from yours? Repent of any jealousy, and thank God for how you have been blessed through the gifts of others. Write down your prayer.

4. **Pray:** *Our Father, thank you that I have purpose in your kingdom. Thank you for those you have placed around me and for their gifts. Forgive me for my self-focused views and for forgetting I am part of a global, heavenly, and eternal kingdom. Expand my heart and renew my mind.*
(Spend a few minutes praying for missionaries around the world.)

> *...so in Christ we who are many form one body, and each member belongs to all the others.*
> —Romans 12:5

**WEEK FIVE
DAY TWO**

"Looks to me as if God provided your *daily bread* today in a generous way," Josh remarked as we rested again on a chapel bench later that day.

I wasn't sure what Josh meant, so I asked, "With this iced tea and cookie you brought me?"

"True, they are a gift from him, but I was thinking of the bigger meaning of *bread*. Perhaps in the Lord's Prayer Jesus uses the word to mean everything we need to sustain our lives here on earth."

"I think I've been praying that prayer all my life without a clue as to what I was really saying. What do you mean?"

"You first," Josh invited. "Tell me about your afternoon. I can see some of the results—they're beautiful; but tell me about the process."

"Well, I don't know why I'm surprised that the people you introduced me to were excited about working on my projects. Ryan is a finish carpenter, and Alex knows how to weld. They must spend some time at the gym. That solid wood mantle looked like a piece of Styrofoam in their arms. Ryan's artistic wife, Anna, took bits of glass, metal, and glazed tile and added decorative interest to the coal bucket firebox. Understated elegance."

> *Trash becoming beautiful—an awesome thing to watch.*

"An elegant coal bucket?" Josh considered what I'd said. "That takes creative genius. But, I can already see how she's making it happen. Trash becoming beautiful—an awesome thing to watch."

"I had a chance to hear each of their stories, Josh. They've experienced healing of their mistakes and regrets. It's as if they were on the road to nowhere, and God rescued them. Ryan said he now uses God's GPS, the Bible, and he's had experiences he never would have had otherwise. He and Anna had been driven by making names for themselves and building a bigger shop. They said their marriage was almost dead until God came into the picture. I loved what Anna said, 'Now instead of asking "What can we get out of this?" we ask, "What can we give?" ' That's why they're here."

Josh was a great listener, and his nod encouraged me to continue. "Alex figured out ways to expand on my ideas. I wanted to cut the mantle in half lengthwise for the front and back of the table. He suggested a different proportion and figured out a way to cut the pillar in long quarters for

> *He said he used to have a list of what he wanted to do before he died. Now he calls it 'what I want to give before I die'.*

legs. He'd also seen a plank that would work for the top of the table, between the mantle pieces.

"Alex is an interesting guy. A lover of architecture, he spent his time-off traveling and studying old buildings. Since he's become a *kingdom resident*—" I gave Josh a sidelong glance, "have you been talking to him, Josh?—he finds places around the world where mission groups can use his skills, and combines helping others with his travel.

"He said he used to have a list of what he wanted to do before he died. Now he calls it 'what I want to give before I die.' I guess you could say God fed me physically and spiritually this afternoon."

The sun's change of position was beginning to give an air of mystery to the mountains. Josh offered me another cookie, stood up, and put his shoe on the bench, as if he needed to stretch. He gave me a minute to savor the chocolate chunks and macadamia nuts in the cookie and then asked, "Taylor, early this afternoon when you realized you couldn't make these projects happen on your own, what were you saying to yourself?"

"Well, thoughts along the line of, 'I'm a weakling,' 'I'm a failure,' 'I'm going to disappoint Josh.'"

"And the focus of those thoughts?"

"I guess on myself—'I, I, I'—on what I can't do and who I am not."

"What if you had said something different?" Josh proposed. "Something like, 'Father God, these ideas you've given me are wonderful. Thank you for your vision. Now I ask you for the way, for the means to make them happen. I don't know the next step. I'm dependent on you.'"

"Well, then I guess I'd be almost like Billy Graham!" Sometimes things like that just slip out, and I'm not sure whether to be amused or apologize. Josh chuckled, then gave me his "no, really" look.

So I thought about it. "Well, I wouldn't have been down on myself and overwhelmed. I could have gone about doing the parts I was able to do, trusting that God would show up. It would have been like saying, 'If this is going to happen, it's up to you, God.'"

"Think what your life would be like if you had that daily dependency on

God, Taylor. Why don't you grab your Bible and ask God to reveal his GPS for your provision."

"I'm going to need X-ray vision. God seems to see needs beneath the surface I didn't even know I had."

If this is going to happen, it's up to you, God.

REFLECT

Just as our physical bodies are dependent on the heart to pump blood and on the brain to tell our knees to bend when we walk, we are dependent on one another in the church, community, and family. Just as children are reliant on parents, as kingdom residents, we are reliant on Father God to meet our needs. This is God's plan and his design.

1. **Read Exodus 16:1-30. Pray:** *God, my Provider, I ask for the Holy Spirit to apply these Scriptures to my life. I don't know everything that will happen or what my needs will be in the next twenty-four hours, but you do. Give me truths and insight to guide me. May I take it in as bread from your hand and heart. Amen.*

From these verses:

Truths God wants to show me:

1.

2.

3.

4.

Practical applications of the truth to my life:

1.

2.

3.

4.

In praying for our daily bread, we are asking God to provide for our immediate needs. The Exodus scripture vividly shows us that God cares about our physical needs and that he longs for us to trust him as the provider of emotional and spiritual needs as well.

2. "I've always lived thinking I've got to figure it out and do it on my own," Taylor would say. Ask God if there are ways you are living like this. If so, pray:

Father God, forgive me for believing it's all up to me. I realize I'm not trusting you in these ways:

Am I unrealistic about what I really need?
Wait and listen. Write down what you think God is saying.

What is the truth?
Wait and listen.

Is there "manna" you have for me today I need to collect? Show me in a way I can understand.

May I choose to believe you will give me today just what I need for today. And may I leave tomorrow in your hands. In Jesus' name, Amen.

WEEK FIVE
DAY THREE   REFLECT

> **Bread:** food in general; support of life in general (Webster); everything we need physically and spiritually.

In our culture of abundance, it is sometimes difficult to tell the difference between needs and wants. *Upgrade, brand-new, top-of-the-line*—we are geared to want more and better. We quickly become discontent as we look at ads or admire what others have. Our needs are often comfortably met, and yet, we are not satisfied. We choose to live with debt, stress, and an endless wish list.

1. **Read 1 Timothy 6:6-10 and 17-19. DIG DEEPER with 6:6–19.**
   a) What will eventually happen to our material goods and accomplishments?

   b) What are 4 reasons Paul gives us to honor God and be content?
   1.

   2.

   3,

   4.

   c) If God chooses to entrust us with more than we need, according to Paul, what should we do?

> **Contentment:** that disposition of mind in which one is, through grace, independent of outward circumstances, so as not to be moved by envy (James 3:16), anxiety (Matthew 6:24, 34), and discontent (1 Corinthians 10:10); satisfaction with what one has (*Unger*).

d) Ask God if your heart has been seduced by the love of money and how this has affected your ability to be content. Write it down.

2. **Read Philippians 4:10-13.**
   a) Does discontent tend to creep into your life because you don't have what you need or because you don't have what you want? Ask the Lord for his perspective.

   b) Sometimes the desire for more possessions is really a yearning to fill an empty place in our hearts. How does **Hebrews 13:5** encourage you to keep your thinking in line with God's?

   c) Ask God to personalize the "secret of being content in any and every situation" (Philippians 4:12). What does it look like for you?

3. Thank the Lord for one insight he gave through these scriptures. May it be daily bread for you today. Write down your prayer.

WEEK FIVE
DAY FOUR   REFLECT

1. **Read John 6:30-35.** Ask God to give you insight into why Jesus calls himself the "bread of life." Write down at least four comparisons between the two:

Physical Bread	Spiritual Bread
1.	1.
2.	2.
3.	3.
4.	4.

2. **Read John 6:46-51.** Once again Jesus' words take us from what we think we want to what we need—from an earthly perspective to a kingdom perspective. The word *believes* in verse 47 means "continues to believe" and signifies an ongoing trust in Jesus. How does this relate to asking God for our daily bread?

Jesus was born in Bethlehem (*Beth* means "house" and *Lehem* means "bread"). He came from heaven to make provision or to be bread for those of us on earth. Jesus offers us his life. He is the bridge between the natural and the spiritual. He is the eternal bread that satisfies.

3. **Read John 6:27.** We saw in Exodus (Week Five, Day Two) that if more manna was collected than needed, it became full of maggots and smelled. Ask God where you are working for things that will "spoil" or are not needed. Ask God where your focus is and if your daily priorities are his.

Respond to him in prayer. Write it down.

Do not work for food that spoils, but for food that endures to eternal life, which the Son of Man will give you. On him God the Father has placed his seal of approval.
—John 6:27

WEEK FIVE
DAY FIVE   REFLECT

The people talking to Jesus in John 6:31-32 thought Moses had provided the manna in the desert. Jesus explained to them it was a provision from God. What about us? Do we attribute our bank account, cars, meals, etc. to our hard work and planning? Do we take personal credit for the blessings in our lives?

> *Don't be deceived, my dear brothers. Every good and perfect gift is from above, coming down from the Father of the heavenly lights, who does not change like shifting shadows.*
> —James 1:16-17

We are often deceived and forget to thank our Heavenly Father for the many ways he provides. What if everything we haven't thanked God for was removed from our lives?

What if everything we haven't thanked God for was removed from our lives?

KINGDOM LAB:
1. Turn on some worship music and spend a few minutes praising God.

2. **Read Psalm 107:1-9** (**DIG DEEPER** and read the entire psalm). Personalize these verses by praying:
   a) *Father, I come to you today to give thanks, for you are good. Your love endures forever. Thank you for providing for my daily physical needs* (list all the Lord brings to mind).

b) *Thank you for all the ways you provide for me spiritually, especially for Jesus and the difference he makes in my life* (list all the Lord brings to mind).

4. **Read Psalm 136** and then personalize it to your life by writing a psalm from your heart to God:

Give thanks to the Lord, for he is good, his love endures forever.
To him who:

> *his love endures forever.*
> *To him who:*

> *his love endures forever.*
> *To him who:*

> *his love endures forever.*
> *To him who:*

> *his love endures forever.*
> *Give thanks to the God of heaven, his love endures forever.*

5. Does this help you realize how much the Father loves you? Spend time soaking in his presence. Be silent. Open your heart and receive his love Record your experience.

WEEK SIX	As we got up from the dinner table, I asked Josh, "Do
DAY ONE	I need to change the sheets in my room before I leave

tomorrow?"

"Tomorrow? I thought you were staying until Sunday. I know we didn't have trout or that great zucchini casserole tonight, but when you asked for seconds I assumed you liked the cannelloni."

"The trout and zucchini principle has proven true in every experience I've had here, Josh. I can't tell you how much it's meant to me. But what I learned about God as our provider encouraged me to think of others more often and to be more generous. This place feels like a five-star resort, and it must cost a fortune to keep it going. I'd like to sponsor a teen on our church's summer mission trip, and I imagine the price of staying here one night would about cover that. See, you've taught me well."

"Hmm, let me stop by the office and get your bill," Josh said. "Then you can see if tomorrow night would be in your budget. I'll meet you out back near the lilac bushes. There are a couple of chairs where we can watch the Creator paint the sky. Should be great viewing this evening."

The sun had just disappeared behind the mountains when Josh joined me. I could tell we were going to be treated to a work of art in the heavens. God seemed so real here. And so good.

"Here's your bill, Taylor. See what you think."

I had been right. In fact, a night's stay was even more than I'd expected. I knew it included meals and my own personal teacher and activities director. *Maybe I should have only stayed one night.*

I glanced at the bottom of the bill and realized it didn't make sense. *What was that last entry: "Transfer to Josh's account"?* There was a zero balance and a handwritten note in the corner:

I've got this one covered, Josh

> *God seemed so real here.*
> *And so good.*

I was confused and glanced at Josh, "I don't get it. It looks like it's being billed to you. That's not right; I can pay it."

"Hey, Friend, it's on me," Josh said. "Will you stay another night? I'll take care of it, too." Josh looked me in the eye.

What is going on? I don't understand. "Why are you doing this for me, Josh? I just met you yesterday. I thought you were the gardener, an employee...who helps misdirected souls like me."

Pausing to soak in the bright pink and orange of the sunset, we sat for a minute or two before Josh replied, "I am a volunteer gardener here. I have the privilege of pruning and planting in both the natural and the spiritual realms. Along with digging in the earth, I do some weeding and seed planting in the minds and hearts of the Father's guests."

"You volunteer? That's awesome! But paying for my room as well? That's too much."

"Most guests contribute what they can for their stay, but sometimes I sense God asking me to put someone's visit on my account—to use the money he's entrusted to me for them."

"Thanks, Josh. I'm truly indebted to you. I don't know what I can do to pay you back. Do you need any design work...anything at all?"

"Taylor, it's a gift. Your bill will be cancelled. The balance is on my account."

"But it's so generous of you. I've got to do something."

"It looks as if there's one more Lord's Prayer insight for you tonight. Are you up for it?" As I nodded, Josh said, "When we say, 'Forgive us our debts,' we're not talking about a monetary debt like a hotel bill. But the idea is similar.

> *Resentment, pride, passivity, anger, and self-pity are like forbidden fruit, and yet we sometimes feast on them.*

"You think what I'm doing is extraordinary. Have you considered the debt you owe God that has already been paid?"

"Sure, I confessed my sin when I became a Christian, and I know Jesus covered that sin with his death on the cross."

"And now you always live a Christ-like life?" Josh asked.

"C'mon, Jesus was perfect." I gave him my "get real" look, but Josh didn't soften the question. So I continued, "I've told you how self-focused I can be and that I tend to ignore God sometimes. Well, maybe a lot. But compared to lots of people—well, I'm usually fairly nice." I really wasn't sure where Josh was going with this.

"What about loving your neighbor as yourself? What about treating your body as a temple of the Holy Spirit? What do you read, watch, or allow to run around in your mind? Are you ever offended or frustrated with someone? Do you always trust God, or do you worry?"

"Who doesn't do those things?" I questioned.

"Only Jesus. But God says to be holy as he is holy. Jesus is our model. One bite of fruit from a tree that was off-limits in the Garden of Eden caused a separation between man and God," explained Josh.

"Resentment, pride, passivity, anger, and self-pity are like forbidden fruit, and yet we sometimes feast on them. We become distanced from God, and the gap gets wide and deep. On our own, there's nothing we can do to make our relationship with God right.

"It's as if we've been sentenced to the basement cell in debtor's prison with no way to earn our freedom and no possibility of pardon. We might as well be dead. And then the jingle of keys is heard. It's Jesus, and he's come to unlock our cell. We follow him up from the pit and out of the prison. He's immediately grabbed and nailed to a waiting cross. 'No! He's not guilty. Stop!' we cry, turning to someone nearby and asking, 'Why? How could this happen?'

"They pronounce, 'It's your fault. He's taking your death sentence; he's paying your debt to society. I guess you can go home.'"

Some things were more clear than they ever had been before. At the same time, new questions muddled my thinking. "That's quite a picture, Josh. Once I'm born again or become a Christian, hasn't my debt been fully paid?"

> *For the wages of sin is death, but the gift of God is eternal life in Christ Jesus our Lord.*
> —Romans 6:23

"Yes, your death warrant has been covered through the blood of Christ. But your salvation is also about recovering from the effects of sin and emotional wounds. It's about spiritual, emotional, and physical wholeness.

"When we are willing to look at negative heart attitudes or actions, and repent, what happens?" Josh questioned. "We get rid of strongholds such as bitterness, fear, anxiety, and anger that block God's love from flowing in and out of us. Confession and receiving God's forgiveness remove the blocks. Living this way, led and empowered by the Holy Spirit, we'll find we repeat those behaviors less and less, and then hopefully not at all as God refines us."

> *For by that one offering he* (Jesus) *perfected forever all those he is making holy.*
> —Hebrews 10:14

Gray and purple clouds made the sunset dramatic, and I soaked it up as I thought about Josh's words. "It's making more sense. But won't looking at my attitudes just put the focus on me?"

"Actually, it's quite a phenomenon, my friend. As you ask God to forgive specific things that are getting in the way of your relationship with him and others, you become more aware of how dependent you are on your Father and how loving and gracious he is.

"Since it's still early, you have time to take these study sheets and your Bible and find a place to talk with God. Until you experience the extent of your debt, you won't experience the fullness of God's love."

I glanced over what Josh had given me. A sense of foreboding was filling my gut. I didn't want to think about my sins. "When you learn what really goes on inside my head, you'll probably send me home tonight—with a bill. This is scary."

"I'll catch up with you in the chapel in a couple of hours. I think we're going to give that firebox a trial run."

Yes, your death warrant has been covered through the blood of Christ. But your salvation is also about recovering from the effects of sin and emotional wounds. It's about spiritual, emotional, and physical wholeness.

"So you're the one who's going to heap burning coals on someone's head—most likely mine—after seeing what I'm really like."

"*To know, know, know you, is to love, love, love you...*" Josh couldn't carry a tune tonight either, and I didn't care. I wanted to be more like him.

REFLECT

Debt: 1) That which is owed from one person to another, whether money, goods, or services; 2) In Scripture: sin; trespass; crime; that which renders liable to punishment (*Webster*).

Once we become Christians, why are we still concerned about our sin or debts?

1. **Read Hosea 10:12.** Unplowed ground is often crusty, hard, or full of weeds. It has to be plowed or prepared before seeds can germinate, take root, and thrive.

a) If the unplowed ground represents our hearts when we have not acknowledged our sin, what is Hosea's warning?

b) What blessings come when we break up the unplowed ground?

2. **Read 1 Peter 1:13-16.** List 5 instructions Peter gives in these verses:

1.

2.

3.

4.

5.

Being holy means being dedicated to God and having his priorities and qualities in our lives.

3. **Read 1 Peter 1:17-21.**

a) From what were we redeemed?

b) What did it cost God?

God's command, "Be holy because I am holy," shows his desire to protect us from an empty way of life.

> *Godly sorrow brings repentance that leads to salvation and leaves no regret, but worldly sorrow brings death.*
> —2 Corinthians 7:10

Godly sorrow leads to repentance, deliverance from sin, and healing so we become more Christ-like. We are left with gratitude for God's grace, something we know we don't deserve but certainly don't regret receiving.

Worldly sorrow is self-centered sadness or regret over the consequences of sin. We are often left with guilt, bitterness, resentment, and shame, which keep us from the abundant life God has for us.

4. **Read 2 Corinthians 7:10 again.**

a) Write down any new insights you have about this verse.

b) Godly sorrow is a gift. Will you allow the Holy Spirit to bring conviction and grace to you this week?

5. God wants us to live in the love, truth, and power that Jesus had while on earth. Sin prevents this from happening and breaks relationship with God and with others. Respond to today's Scriptures in a written prayer.

WEEK SIX
DAY TWO   REFLECT

As Christians, we look at our debt to see if there is anything blocking our relationship with God. We can start with the Ten Commandments.

1. **Read Deuteronomy 5:6-21**. Ask God to show you the truth and write down specifics.

a) "You shall have no other gods before me." Have you ever made anything or anyone a higher priority than God? Be specific.

b) "You shall not make for yourself an idol..." Have you ever placed a movie star, athlete, church leader, child, accomplishment, or possession as a higher priority than God?

c) "You shall not misuse the name of the Lord your God..." In what ways have you misrepresented his name by using profanity, by casual use, by ignoring his authority, or by not thanking him or asking him for wisdom?

d) "Remember the Sabbath day by keeping it holy." In what ways do you take time to rest, acknowledging God's place in your life? Do you give God one-seventh of your time?

e) Do you honor your father and mother, ever have a lustful thought, murder others by your judgments, steal from God and others by not tithing or sharing what he's entrusted to you, speak critical words, or envy a belonging or trait of another?

2. Read Matthew 5:21-22 and Hebrews 4:12-13.
God's Word says the commandments are not only about our actions, but also about our _____.

The commandments show us that we are sinners. How can we ever hope to have a close relationship with God? How can we live holy lives?
In the Lord's Prayer, Jesus says we are to ask our Father—the Creator, the Almighty One—to forgive us.

Forgive: to pardon; to forsake the right to punish the crime, offense or debt; to cancel or send away.

3. Respond to God in a written prayer. Feel the weight of your indebtedness. If you don't understand the debt, you won't understand your need for a Savior—and you won't understand his love.

> *If you don't understand the debt, you won't understand your need for a Savior—and you won't understand his love.*

WEEK SIX
DAY THREE   REFLECT

If we honestly look at how Jesus calls us to live, we realize that apart from him, we have the potential of being the worst of sinners. The sense of "I'm basically a pretty good person" shifts to "without Christ I would be a scary person."

Just as the attitude of "I'm not so bad" is not biblical, neither is "I'm totally unworthy." We are not to live in condemnation or shame.

1. **Read Luke 7:36-50.**

   a) Do you ever feel a close relationship with Jesus is not possible for you? If so, why?

   b) In this Scripture, what was Jesus' perspective? Did he think the prostitute or the religious leaders would love him more and be better able to receive his love? Why?

2. **Read Matthew 26:26-28.** Jesus' blood was shed for the forgiveness of sins. Are you willing to believe once and for all that Christ's sacrifice is *bigger* than your sin? Are you willing to admit how much you need a Savior?

PRAY: *Jesus, you gave me the gift of forgiveness. You covered my debt with your sacrifice on the cross. Please forgive me for thinking it's not for me—for thinking I need to do more so I'll be able to receive it—for thinking I'm the exception because my sin is so great.*

Forgive me, too, for times I think I don't really need you, for forgetting what you have done for me, for not rejoicing over the gift of my salvation every day.

I come to you with my alabaster jar representing gratefulness for all you've done for me and love for who you are. As I pour it out on you, what do you do or say to me?

Tell Jesus you receive his forgiveness and love. Write it out.

I reject the lie that I am unworthy. What is the truth, Lord?

I take up the truth. Thank you that I'm beginning to see how much I have been forgiven. Thank you for:

May my understanding be transformed into love for you, Jesus, and for others. Amen.

WEEK SIX
DAY FOUR   REFLECT

A personal revival begins with conviction of our sin, repentance, and a sincere desire to live in obedience to God. In Day Two's lesson, you probably saw specific sins needing confession. Continue the process today, and tomorrow we will use the list in a Kingdom Lab.

1. **Read Psalm 24:1-6.** Write a prayer using this Scripture or pray:
Lord, I want to stand in your presence—to have nothing get in the way of my relationship with you. Use today's lesson to prepare the way for me to have clean hands and a pure heart. I seek your face, O God of Jacob. Amen.

2. **Read Colossians 3.** Ask God to use this chapter to show you ways you are not honoring God, others, or yourself. Look at verse 15. If we do not have peace, perhaps it is a sign of sin. Are you holding on to blame, wanting your own way, or not trusting God? Ask God if a lack of peace in any circumstance in your life is a warning sign.

3. Make a list of unconfessed sins. You do not have to dig for them. Simply use this week's lesson and ask God to reveal to you anything that is getting in the way of receiving and giving his love.

My debts:

4. **Read Psalm 24:7-10** out loud several times—until you are filled with assurance that the King of glory is mightier than any sin and that he will come in and complete the good work he's begun in you (Philippians 1:6). Write a response to God.

**WEEK SIX
DAY FIVE**

Standing before the chapel cross under the starlit sky, I felt so small. I held my list of debts owed to God—those things I'd done or left undone, the judgments I'd made toward others, the superiority I sometimes felt, my prejudices, the behaviors and choices I justify...

Josh already had coals lit in the firebox. So far the iron grate stand was stable, and no sparks were escaping from the coal bucket. Some talented people had helped pull that project off.

"Taylor, go ahead and read your list of debts out loud. We'll use the James 5:16 model, '...confess your sins to one another and pray for each other so that you may be healed.'"

> *Standing before the chapel cross under the starlit sky, I felt so small.*

"Out loud? Here? In front of you?"

"Everyone needs help. What you say here won't be repeated to anyone else. It's a safe place, Taylor."

I looked behind me to see if anyone else had come into the chapel and then back down at my list. The word *pride* jumped out at me—as if it were highlighted and in bold type. I cleared my throat and glanced up at Josh, "Okay, here goes." Starting at the top of my list, I began, "God, I've learned you are a good Father. I'm sorry I've let so many things get in the way of knowing you more. I've come tonight with debts I have no way of repaying, asking for your mercy.

"I admit I often think the TV will be better company than you. I've spent a lot of time trying to get ahead of people—at work, on the roads, in the grocery store. I've been critical and have spent my fair share of time gossiping. I've been holding resentment toward..."

When I'd read the whole list, I looked up at Josh. "Taylor," Josh said, "just tell God you repent and ask him to forgive you. He sees your heart."

It took a life to make a way for me to be right with God, the life of the only perfect man.

"I repent and ask you to forgive me, Father God. I don't want to live this way anymore."

"Now nail your list to the cross," Josh directed.

I picked up the hammer and nail, and the sound of my pounding echoed off the hills. *It took a life to make a way for me to be right with God, the life of the only perfect man.* A sense of grief came over me, and I set the hammer down, then looked over at Josh.

"I want to change—to live differently—but I'm afraid I won't. I've struggled with some of these things for a long time."

Josh nodded, and like a big brother, put his arm around me. "Have you ever told anyone else about those struggles? Have you ever asked anyone else to pray with you?"

I want to change—to live differently—but I'm afraid I won't. I've struggled with some of these things for a long time.

I shook my head "no." *Why would I risk further embarrassment? You should just keep those things to yourself.*

Glancing at the firebox, Josh continued, "Remember this afternoon when you realized you couldn't build this on your own? You were in a much better spot than when you were trying to do it by yourself. Why don't you tell God you can't do it on your own; you're dependent on him?"

"Right now?"

"Sure, go ahead," Josh encouraged.

"Umm, Father God, I want to change, but I don't really know if I can. Would you change me? Show me how to cooperate with you. I guess I need the power of the Holy Spirit—and maybe a friend or two—ones like Josh. And—thank you."

"Taylor, did you receive God's forgiveness?"

"Well, I think so. But I can't quite believe it's that simple—that he just gives it to me."

"With your own father, you felt you had to earn love, didn't you? His approval cost you something. It's not that way with God."

"It's not that way with you either, Josh. You paid the bill for my stay here. I did nothing to earn it."

"You could have refused it, though, Taylor—said something like, 'I'm going to do it on my own,' or let pride or perhaps unworthiness get in the way. In humility and with gratefulness, you received my gift."

He pulled my list of sins off the cross and placed it in the firebox. "As far as the east is from the west, so far has God removed your sin from you."

Josh looked me in the eyes and said, "Taylor, child of God, you are forgiven. The blood of Christ has cancelled your debt." He pulled my list of sins off the cross and placed it in the firebox. "As far as the east is from the west, so far has God removed your sin from you."

In a few moments, my list was burned, and I marveled at God's love for me. A clean slate—a zero balance. That's extravagant love. *God, teach me to love this way.*

Soon I heard Josh rustling in his backpack. *What was he looking for? Were those marshmallows he was pulling out? And chocolate and graham crackers?*

"S'mores? In the chapel?" I couldn't quite believe my eyes.

"Celebrating the goodness of God is a reverent thing to do. Let's see if this firebox roasts a good marshmallow. And since it's a joyful occasion, do you want me to sing—s'more?"

Once again, I rolled my eyes. I did feel like celebrating. *From regret to roasting marshmallows—I'd like my dad to experience this.*

REFLECT

KINGDOM LAB:
If you have never confessed your sins with another person, consider going through this lab with a trusted friend.

We will follow Taylor's forgiveness experience at The Father's House. In prayer, picture yourself standing before a cross. Pray out loud:

God, I've learned you are a good Father. I'm sorry I've let so many things get in the way of knowing you more. I come today with debts I have no way of repaying, asking for your mercy (not receiving what is deserved).
I admit (read your list of sins from Day Four's lesson):

I repent and ask you to forgive me, Father God. I don't want to live this way anymore.

In prayer, picture nailing your list of sins to the cross. Reflect on what your sin cost Jesus. Write down what comes to mind.

Ask the Holy Spirit to empower you to live differently.

If you're praying with another person, have him or her speak forgiveness to you. If not, receive it in prayer from God.
_____ (your name), *child of God, you are forgiven. The blood of Jesus Christ has cancelled your debt.*

Tell God you receive his forgiveness and picture your list being burned or disappearing in some way. Write down what you sense happens to your list.

Read Psalm 103:10-12. Thank God for his extravagant love. Write down your praise.

Look again at the story of the prodigal son and the merciful father in **Luke 15:11-24.** The father's response to the son's returning home is Father God's response to you. Walk toward the Father in prayer. Look at him. Let him look at you. What is his response? Are you able to receive it? Write out your experience.

> *And when you were dead in your transgressions and the uncircumcision of your flesh, he made you alive together with him, having forgiven us all our transgressions, having cancelled out the certificate of debt consisting of decrees against us and which was hostile to us; and he has taken it out of the way, having nailed it to the cross.*
> —Colossians 2:13-14, *(NASV)*

WEEK SEVEN

As We Forgive Our Debtors

WEEK SEVEN One for the pail, one to eat, one for the pail, one to
DAY ONE eat. It would take awhile to pick enough strawberries
for pies at this speed, but the berries were irresistible.
Josh was over on the next row, and I asked him if I had a time limit.

"Just save enough for the pies," Josh answered as he popped a berry in
his mouth. "We've got quite a group coming to the banquet tonight."

I'd noticed more people at The Father's House this morning. "What's
going on?" I asked.

"We often have groups here on Saturday and sometimes Sunday. They
either come to help out or for a retreat. On weekends we tend to have
more drop-ins, like you, not really sure why they've come at first."

So I'm not the only one. "It probably doesn't take them long to figure
out it's part of a plan they didn't even know was in play, and they have a
leading role. I'll keep my eyes open for any with 'deer in the headlight'
looks and tell them they'll basically be all right..." Josh gave me a warning
glance. "Okay, I won't tell them to watch out for rockslides or zucchini."

As we picked berries, Josh asked me how my night had been.

"I figured it would take awhile to go to sleep with those s'mores
mooshing around inside, but my head connected with the pillow, and I
was out. Do you think that knowing you're forgiven can be a sleep-aid?"

"Maybe we could market that and use the profits for a new guest house. What do you think?"

"I think you should keep on with your day job, Josh." He gave me a thumbs-up, and I continued. "Before breakfast I looked over the Lord's Prayer again, and it seems to me God's forgiveness is conditional. Last night things seemed clear, and now it's as if there's a catch. Can you pick and talk at the same time?"

Do you think knowing you're forgiven can be a sleep-aid?

"*Pick-a-little, talk-a-little, pick-a-little, talk-a-little, pick, pick, pick...*"

I joined in Josh's off-key song for a few seconds and then told him I'd try to be more careful of my wording. "Sure I can pick and talk," he said. "What do you see as the condition, or *catch*, as you called it?"

"Jesus says to ask God to forgive us in the same way we forgive others. I read the next couple of verses, and Jesus goes on to say if we don't forgive others, God won't forgive us. That's not very loving in my opinion."

"So you think that requirement goes against the character of God—against the nature of a loving Father?"

Where did Josh come up with these twists to my thoughts? "At first glance, I do. But I think you're here to revamp my mind—and so far I've been appreciative."

Josh checked my pail, "Let's finish picking these two rows, and then we should have enough for pies. So Taylor, what would you say holding on to unforgiveness does for people?"

"Probably nothing good. But come on, Josh. Some things are impossible to forgive. What about the drunk driver who kills your spouse? What about the fathers who abuse children, a rapist who steals innocence and trust, a mother who leaves home for another man? What about betrayal, untrue accusations, extortion? Some things are big and deserve punishment."

So Taylor, what would you say holding on to unforgiveness does for people?

Josh kept picking, and I figured I'd stumped him. After a couple of minutes, he said, "Actually, we're not talking about removing consequences for behavior. We have policemen and courts of law to help maintain order, to protect us, and hopefully to help people get back on track. But do you know anyone who seems to be...bitter, for instance?"

When Josh said "bitter," one of my aunts immediately came to mind. She was a wonderful woman, but she had never gotten over the fact that she'd lost a baby boy to a rare virus. His name was Toby and she was convinced the doctors could have done more to save him. My aunt was hard for me to be around, as if her other kids and I were supposed to make up for what she'd lost. She was somehow stuck in that moment of her life—for the rest of her life.

I told Josh what had come to mind, and he nodded. "Life does have tough places that are difficult to move beyond. Yet, her unforgiveness of the doctors, of God, and probably of herself stole joy and contentment from her. That's what Jesus is talking about—the condition of our hearts. He's teaching us more about our loving Father who wants to protect us from poisoning our hearts and minds. Unforgiveness is an open invitation to Satan: 'Come on over! I've got some fertile soil for anger, resentment, and bitterness. Go ahead and plant!' It will destroy us and those around us as well as our relationship with God. It's that serious, Taylor."

"I've got some mulling over to do, Josh. I think I'm ready for more Scriptures to help this mind-renewal scheme of yours."

"No problem, Taylor. That was on the morning's plan. Let's take these berries to the kitchen."

Walking back to The Father's House with our pails in hand, Josh said, "I've learned a little about your father and his impact on you, but tell me about your mother. What was your relationship with her like?"

> *Unforgiveness is an open invitation to Satan: 'Come on over! I've got some fertile soil for anger, resentment, and bitterness. Go ahead and plant!'*

"As we were talking back in the strawberry field, she came to mind."

"Do you have unforgiveness toward her?"

"I'll have to think about that. Yesterday I would have said 'no' but I'm learning I don't really know what's going on in my heart without asking God. My heart can have a mind of its own.

"I remembered making strawberry jam with my mom, and realize that the times of just doing something simple with her didn't happen very often. She was either too busy or else in bed with migraines. I know she couldn't help it, but I guess I still feel cheated."

"What did you miss out on, do you think?"

"I would have liked to have been able to talk things over with Mom. You know, simple things like trouble at recess when I was young; and as I got older, the things my friends were doing that were confusing to me and my craving to fit in. She worried a lot. I don't think I left the house once without hearing, 'Be careful.' She probably looked at herself in the mirror every morning and whispered, 'Be careful!'"

> *Most people need to admit that their parents missed seeing their hearts, realize what it cost them, and then forgive.*

Josh looked at me with a wry smile, and simply nodded.

"A lot of times she was sick and just unavailable. Maybe that's one reason I have a good imagination—lots of time on my own."

"That's tough for a kid, but you're not alone. Most people need to admit that their parents missed seeing their hearts, realize what it cost them, and then forgive."

Back at the kitchen, Josh exchanged my pail for study sheets and a sack lunch. "There's a place to go through the steps of forgiveness on these pages. Find me when you're done."

"I think I'll walk across the log over the creek and find a spot to nestle into."

"If only your mother could see you now. Be sure to wear a helmet and a life preserver, and whatever you do..."

"I know. Be careful!"

REFLECT

God is in the process of advancing his kingdom on earth through Christians. He has put his Spirit within us and is remolding us into his image. Are you soft and moldable? Are you willing to learn how to truly forgive, not just say the words? As we make the choice to forgive and work through the pain, we become more like Jesus. Forgiveness is not a suggestion; it is a mandate for kingdom living.

Will you give God permission to change your way of thinking this week if necessary?

Pray: *Father God, yes. You have permission to change my thinking in any place it does not line up with the Bible. I realize I have some apprehension because:*

Remove any wrong ideas or lies I've believed. I want to live in the freedom of your truth. Amen.

You might be saying, "Fine, I'll go through the motions, but you don't know about my pain—about what was done to me. I don't know how I can ever let it go." Will you take courage, walk through this week's lesson, and trust God? He is a gentle Father and understands your heart. He won't desert you in your pain. Stay close to him. He's good. And he sees you.

> *Therefore, prepare your minds for action; be self-controlled; set your hope fully on the grace to be given you when Jesus Christ is revealed.*
> —1 Peter 1:13

1. **Read Matthew 6:14-15** and write it down.

a) Ask the Holy Spirit to reveal why this contingency clause is included.

b) Respond to God in prayer.

WEEK SEVEN
DAY TWO   REFLECT

Injustice: A wrong; treatment that was not deserved; unmerited blame.

Two possible responses to injustice:
1. **Justice:** giving what is due; vindictive retribution; merited punishment.
2. **Mercy:** withholding due punishment; that benevolence or tenderness of heart which disposes a person to overlook injuries or to treat an offender better than he deserves; the disposition that induces an injured person to forgive trespasses; pardon (Webster).

1. **Read Matthew 5:7.**
   a) What are some ways this message clashes with our culture?

   b) How does this verse relate to the Lord's Prayer?

We often want mercy for ourselves but justice for others. The kingdom of God does not operate that way, but rather by the principles:

Do you want mercy or justice from God?

- Treat others as you want to be treated (from Matthew 7:12).
- Love your neighbor as yourself (from Mark 12:31).
- A man reaps what he sows (Galatians 6:7).

Do you want mercy or justice from God?

2. **Read Luke 15:25-32**, the conclusion of the prodigal son story.

a) By whom is the oldest son offended, and why?

b) How did the offense affect his heart and relationships?

c) If the older son had understood the mercy he had been given from God, what would he have said about his brother's return and the celebration? Ask God to show you.

d) Do you ever feel as if you are overlooked or taken for granted, perhaps by others or by God? Read verse 31. What was the father saying?

e) Does your heart condition sometimes cause you to miss what God has for you? Respond to God in a written prayer.

WEEK SEVEN
DAY THREE   REFLECT

God seems to say to us, "Now if you want to live in this place of receiving my full forgiveness, you must be forgiving. That is the deal. You cannot ask for mercy for yourself and judgment for others."

1. **Read Matthew 18:21-35**, the parable of the unmerciful servant.

a) **Read Genesis 4:24**. Man's natural desire for revenge and resentment is being reversed by Jesus—first as he teaches the truth and then later through the empowering gift of the Holy Spirit in us.

b) Look at **Matthew 18:25**. Take a moment and think how you would feel if the penalty for your debt was your family being sold into slavery—and all that slavery might require. Write it down.

c) What did the servant do (verse 26)?

d) How would you feel toward the king who totally cancelled your debt—who said in effect, "You owe, but I'll pay"?

e) The servant doesn't seem to grasp that he received even more than he asked for. What was the condition of his heart?

f) What did the king expect of the servant?

g) In life, what are some *torturers*—physically, emotionally, and spiritually—of unforgiveness?

h) Ask the Lord how unforgiveness has *tortured* you? Be specific.

If we don't extend forgiveness to others, we really don't understand what we have received from God. If anything seems *too much to forgive,* we believe that Jesus' death on the cross wasn't enough for our sin or for that of another. We need to repent of pride—of thinking we know better than God.

2. Respond to today's study in a written prayer.

WEEK SEVEN DAY FOUR It took me awhile to find Josh. He was up on a ladder in the orchard examining a tree.

"What do you see up there?" I called.

Poking his head up between the branches, Josh looked me over. "Well, besides seeing a friend who's returned safely from a dangerous mission without a helmet—" he smirked, pretending to look shocked, "—what would your mother say?"

I rolled my eyes and smiled as Josh got back to business, "I'm trying to see if these trees survived the frost we had a week ago. Even one below-freezing night, and they won't yield what they're supposed to."

> *I had no idea unforgiveness and judgments have so many consequences.*

Coming down the ladder, Josh asked, "How did it go with you? I sent you off with a lot to think about." Looking to my right, he asked, "How 'bout a seat on these hay bales?"

"Sure, I want to talk over part of this study with you. I had no idea unforgiveness and judgments have so many consequences. It's as if the very things I judged in my mother are playing out in my life. I have trouble believing others will really be there for me or that I'm even worth spending time with. What a cycle!"

"I can see how that pattern played out in my family. Like my dad, my mom did the best she knew how. She didn't realize I often felt rejected or abandoned and that her anxiety kept me from feeling that I could talk with her. Now, I realize, I thought I had to protect her."

"That's a big responsibility for a little kid, Taylor. Not what God intended. Before your study, had you ever thought of something being stolen from you because of your mother's anxiousness and unavailability?"

"That was a new idea to me, but it was powerful."

"Since we're in the orchard, think about this: woundedness can rob us. Just as the frost might steal what this tree was created for, your mother's anxiety deprived you of an open, nurturing relationship with her. I wonder if it's difficult for you to think of the Holy Spirit being a dependable counselor who's always there for you."

"Another effect her own pain had on me. Wow."

"Did you understand that forgiveness isn't saying what she did was okay? She didn't have to live with her fears and most likely could have gotten more help with her health issues. Forgiveness is saying you cancel her debt to you. You let her off the hook for what you missed out on. She owes; Jesus paid; you cancel the debt. Her balance due to you is zero."

"Like my debt to The Father's House."

"Exactly."

The hay was getting a little scratchy, and I stood up, then knelt down near Josh. "It was humbling to see how I'd been holding judgments against my mom, like 'She's weak,' and 'She can't be counted on.' Quite a few times she was supposed to help out at my grade school—drive for field trips, help with the Christmas party—but at the last minute she cancelled because she said she didn't feel well. When stuff like that happened, I swore that when I had children, I'd never let them down like that. That's setting myself up, isn't it? How do I know what I'll be able to do or not do?"

> *Forgiving others is a gift we give ourselves. It opens windows to our heart we didn't even know were shut.*

"Did you ask God to forgive you for your judgments and vows?"

"I did. God showed me that my mom has always wanted a closer relationship with me, but her regret and guilt kept her from reaching out. I think I'm going to call her regularly and put more effort into getting to know her."

"It might be a process, Taylor, but I bet you'll see some changes as a result of your forgiveness."

"God reminded me of another thing. It really sounds corny, but it brought those tears back to my eyes. My mom would make up silly rhymes for me when I was little, and I'd laugh and laugh. I'd say, 'More Mommy, more,' and she'd say another one. *'Tayl, Tayl rides a whale, down the road to get the mail.'* I'd forgotten those times. I think she must have felt better then. I'd forgotten we'd laughed."

"Forgiving others is a gift we give ourselves. It opens windows in our hearts we didn't even know were shut."

My heart seemed to be full of possibility again—and lighter. *Must be an open window or two.*

"Ryan and Anna came by to see if you'd help them finish the Communion table. They said they'd be in the workshop."

I'm not sure what came over me, but I got up, stood on the hay bale,

112

spread my arms out wide and called out, "*Ry, Anna, watch me fly, over to help–look up high!*"

It was Josh's turn to roll his eyes. Then he put his hands on his hips and said, "You're not being careful! You forgot your seatbelt—and your oxygen mask! What are we going to do with you?"

REFLECT

1. **Read Galatians 5:13-15**. Ask God to highlight one part for you. Write it down. Why does God want you to apply this to your thinking or actions?

2. **Read Hebrews 12:15**. What is the warning in this verse, and how does it relate to forgiving others?

3. **Read Matthew 7:1-2**. This is a spiritual law.
   a) How does this spiritual law tie in to the law of sowing and reaping (Galatians 6:7)?

   b) Can you think of any way you judged a parent, for instance, and later found you acted in the same way?

4. Ask God to show you one person you hold unforgiveness or bitterness toward. Today will be the beginning of steps towards forgiveness, and the final steps will be given in *Day Five*.

   a) **Pray**: *God, I ask your Holy Spirit to lead me. Bring to mind someone who has hurt me. I'll trust that is the situation I'm to use in this exercise. Name of person or initial:*

b) *God, help me be specific and real about what he or she did to hurt me.*

c) *What judgment did I make against him or her? Show me my heart, God, and put it into words.*

d) *What vows* (see Matthew 5:33-36) *did I make?* (Consider what you may have taken into your own hands that is only possible through God's strength or authority. Vows can be tied to judgments.)

e) *What effect did this wrong have on me?*

What was stolen from me (for example: honor, nurture, innocence, trust)? Be real. It might not seem rational. That is okay.

f) *What do I think this person owes because of the effect this hurt had on me? What is the debt?* (Be honest. What change would you like to see; what would you like done?) Take time and listen to God. We have to acknowledge and feel the weight of the debt so we'll understand what we are cancelling.

Ask God to continue to bring to mind anything else about this situation that would be helpful in this exercise and write it down. You may want to continue on to Day Five and complete the prayer of forgiveness.

WEEK SEVEN
DAY FIVE   REFLECT

1. **Read Revelation 12:10**. How is Satan described?

When we replay injustices in our mind, thinking about what we could or should have said or done, we are often aligning ourselves with Satan and his ways. We stand accusing the one who hurt us, "It's her fault!" or "He is guilty!"

What if God said to us, "Do you desire mercy and grace (undeserved favor)? If so, are you willing to give up your rights and extend mercy and grace to another? Do not give the evil one an opportunity to steal, kill, and destroy. Extend the gift of forgiveness as I've forgiven you."

Remember that the hurtful things that have happened to you were not Father God's heart. They are a result of the sin of others and sometimes of wrong choices we have made. Know that the sin and its effects are not the end of the story. Our Father is a God who "works in all things for the good of those who love him and who have been called according to his purpose" (Romans 8:28).

2. **KINGDOM LAB:** You have laid the groundwork for prayer. Now invite the presence of the Holy Spirit to be fresh and real. Wait on him. The Holy Spirit will enable you to pray:

> *Father God, you are loving and good. I come to you and ask you to help me pray. I choose mercy over judgment (James 2:13). You have shown me mercy and grace. You have forgiven me a debt I could never repay. No amount of good works or money would ever be enough. Today I want to be set free from the torment and burden of unforgiveness.*

Using Day Four's question (4 a-f), pray out loud:

• *I forgive* (4a) (person's name) *for* (4b) (speak what you have written).

• *Forgive me for making these judgments:* (read 4c). *I break them in the name of Jesus and place the cross of Christ between the judgments and myself. Set me free from ways I've acted or been judged in the same ways.*

• *Forgive me for making these vows:* (read 4d). *I submit to your power and authority in my life and trust you to give me strength to live a life pleasing to you. Set me free from these vows.*

• *I choose to forgive the debt that* (name of person) *owes me. He/she no longer needs to:* (4f) *(for example: apologize, suffer because of what they did to me, make up for it, etc.).*

• *I am not pretending that what happened was okay or right. But I cancel the debt. The balance owed to me is zero. If Satan brings it to mind, I can say, "I've forgiven him/her. You'll have to take it up with God."*

• *I bless* (name of person). *Heavenly Father, would you pour out your love, healing, and goodness on him/her. Would you draw* (name) *close to you. Heal my heart and his/her heart, too, Lord.*

• Now in prayer, walk this person to Jesus and hand him/her over. You are no longer tied to this person through unforgiveness. What does Jesus do?

• Ask Jesus to show you this person as he sees him/her. Write it down.

• Ask Jesus what he says to you. Jot it down. Then see if it relates to Day Four, Question One. Respond to Jesus in a written prayer.

> *"And when you stand praying, if you hold anything against anyone, forgive him, so that your Father in heaven may forgive you your sins."*
> —Jesus' words in Mark 11:25

Lead Us Not Into Temptation

**WEEK EIGHT
DAY ONE** Josh was outfitting me with a headlamp, and I was a little apprehensive about his plan. We had walked for about a half hour from The Father's House, and I'd had a chance to fill him in on my time working on the Communion table project with Ryan, Anna, and Alex. The craftsmen had taken my vision and had embellished it in beautiful ways. The table was a work of art; when I left, they were oiling it to give it some protection from the elements. Yes, I'd seen the body of Christ at work, and it felt good to have been part of a team.

But now it would feel good to stay out in the daylight rather than go into a cave. I didn't want to admit it, but dark, cramped places and I didn't do well together. When I was about eight years old, during a game of hide-and-seek, a couple of the older kids in the neighborhood had triple-dog-dared me to hide under the crawl space of our house. They'd promised to put the cover back over the opening with a guarantee that I would surely be the winner. After about ten minutes of hiding, I'd felt something crawl over me. "A black widow!" my eight-year-old brain shrieked, and I'd frantically scrambled to the opening—which wouldn't budge when I pushed on it. I'm not sure which was worse—the fear of dying from a spider bite or the ridicule the older kids gave me for screaming to get out. But, now, it's all associated with darkness and uncertain escape routes.

> *Trust me, Taylor,*
> *and I'll lead you.*

"So Josh—is there, like, any light in this cave?"

"It's a cave, Taylor," Josh said matter-of-factly.

I shuddered inwardly. "Well, have you ever seen any bats, spiders, or falling rocks in there?"

"No, walking through this cave is a rather tame experience. I figure the serpent that lives in there eats anything that moves."

I gave him my "be serious" look. "Anything small, I mean," he added with a smile.

As we walked towards the mouth of the cave, I imagined how Jonah must have felt being swallowed by the whale. *What would the belly of the cave be like...besides dark?*

"Remind me why we're doing this, Josh."

"Besides because it's there?" Of course I rolled my eyes, and Josh went on, "We still have one more part of the Lord's Prayer to look at, and there's something I want you to see."

"I'm already praying, *'Deliver me, deliver me, deliver me,'* but it doesn't seem to be helping. My legs are following you."

Josh stepped inside the cave. "It's time to turn on our lamps. So, Taylor, what are you afraid of?"

"I've never liked darkness and tight spaces. Maybe that's the downside to a vivid imagination."

"Or maybe God wants to set you free of that fear. Of course there are times to be cautious; but I've been in this cave several times, and we have the proper equipment. Trust me, Taylor, and I'll lead you."

"What did Jesus say?" I asked. "Something about being willing but having weak flesh. That's pretty much how I am."

"But before that, Jesus gave the disciples instructions to 'watch and pray' so they wouldn't fall into temptation. You're feeling the pressure of fear—fear of the unknown—and the temptation is to relieve the pressure by turning around and going back," Josh explained. "You're already watching—being awake and aware of what's going on—so let's pray."

That sounded like a good idea to me and Josh led, "God, our Protector, we reject fear in the name of Jesus Christ and take up the truth: you have not given us a spirit of fear, but a spirit of power, of love, and of self-discipline (I Timothy 1:7). Thank you for the Holy Spirit living in us. We choose to let go of fear today and to replace it with trust in you, God.

You're feeling the pressure of fear— fear of the unknown—and the temptation is to relieve the pressure by turning around and going back.

Do you have anything you'd like Taylor to know?

"Just wait and listen for a minute, Taylor."

> *Watch and pray so that you will not fall into temptation.*
> *The spirit is willing, but the body is weak.*
> —Mark 14:38

I waited, but I wasn't sure about the thought that came to mind. It did bring a chuckle to me, and I looked up at Josh questionably.

"What did you hear?"

"I'm not sure it was God. I heard, 'Yeah, he's a little *out-there*, but you can trust him.' "

"I assume the *him* is me?" I nodded. Josh laughed and shook his head, "God definitely has a sense of humor. That would be his voice, Taylor. Since God is my Father, I guess you could say I'm a *chip off the old block*— my Heavenly Father is a little *out-there* at times, too, in an amazingly, wonderful way. Come on. We've got a cave waiting on us."

Following closely behind Josh, I picked my way through rocks and trickles of water and wound around corners in the cave. *Is this how rats in mazes feel?* After a few more turns, Josh stopped and said, "Okay, I want you to try something. Turn off your light."

"What if it won't go back on?"

"You've got to trust me, Taylor." Josh turned off his light and, once again, I followed. It turned completely black.

"What is the length of this cave? Why isn't there a trace of light?"

"We've zigzagged enough that the light on both ends is blocked. Hold on to my backpack and follow me, in the dark, just for a few minutes. I know this part of the cave well. Okay?"

"No gradual breaking of this fear, I guess."

Every step I took was tentative, and I could tell we were squeezing between a couple of rocks and then taking a turn—and then another. It wasn't long before I told Josh, "I think I'm finally beginning to see in the dark."

"Actually, Taylor, we are seeing light from the other end of the cave. And soon you'll spot a shaft of light from our exit. Go ahead and turn your lamp back on, and follow me."

I was thankful I had brought a sweatshirt. It was cool, but I was more relaxed and now able to look around at the different colors and layers in the rocks. There was beauty there I almost missed.

> *Would you give in to the fear and turn around, or would you trust me to lead you through the darkness?*

We came to the opening in the cave. I looked up to see blue sky and wispy clouds. Josh pointed to a rustic ladder and said, "Go ahead. Climb on out."

The rungs of the ladder supported us despite how weak they looked, and soon we were resting on some flat rocks. Josh pulled trail mix from his pack and passed it to me. "You ruined the plans of the evil one there, Taylor. He is out to steal freedom from you—freedom to be at peace when it's dark—as well as to explore caves, of course."

I smiled. "Of course. That part of the prayer makes sense, but I don't understand why we ask God not to lead us into temptation. What good father would lead his young child to a campfire, say, 'Don't play in the fire,' and walk away? It doesn't make sense."

"You can study more about this before dinner, and I think you will see that the temptation Jesus is talking about is taking things into our own hands rather than trusting God. Life's circumstances test us or put pressure on us.

"Thoughts of walking through a cave caused you to feel the pressure of fear, and you were tested. Would you give in to the fear and turn around, or would you trust me to lead you through the darkness? Because you trusted, you were delivered from fear the evil one could use to cause anxiety."

"Life is full of tests, isn't it, Josh? When you had me turn off my headlamp, there was only blackness. Without you I wouldn't have known which way to go. I see why you had me leave my light off for a few minutes. It's sometimes that way when we're following God, isn't it? It can feel confusing—which way is up?—and that feels like pressure. I often decide I can't take it any longer and grab whatever I can to relieve the stress."

"That's the temptation we're asking God to keep us away from. The evil one wants to stop us from trusting God because, the more we trust God, the less fearful, anxious, and controlling we are."

"You've given me a lot to think about, Josh."

"We'll have a late dinner tonight because of the banquet, so you'll have time to look over the study sheets. I'll come to your room before dinner, and we can talk over any questions that have come up.

"Let's head back. Do you want me to blindfold you and lead you, to work on this trust issue some more?"

Josh reminded me of a swim instructor I had who often pushed a little further than I was comfortable going. "I think you're ready for the diving board, Taylor," and then the next week, "Taylor, you are as graceful as a dolphin—time for the high dive." It wasn't always comfortable, but thanks to her, I'm a good swimmer. No fear there.

> *...the more we trust God, the less fearful, anxious, and controlling we are.*

"You're more than a little out-there, Josh. You're way out-there. And you've shown me a way out of my anxiousness. I think I can skip the blindfold. But Josh, you're out-and-out outstanding, just like your Father."

"I'm going to miss you, Taylor. I think you're a chip off the old block, too."

REFLECT

1. Like Taylor, have you had questions about praying, "Lead us not into temptation..."? What do you think it means?

Peiramos is the Greek word translated "temptation'" in the Lord's Prayer. It can also mean "test" or "pressure." With the words "but deliver us from the evil one," we have the sense that the evil one tries to slink into the test, pressure, or temptation.

> *Will we trust God to work things out, or will we give in to the temptations offered by the evil one?*

Sometimes when we pray the Lord's Prayer in our churches we say, "Deliver us from evil," and we may think we are simply praying for protection from bad things happening to us. This phrase is also translated, "Deliver us from the evil one," and seems to take on a deeper meaning. So many situations in our lives become pressurized, and we have a decision to make: Will we trust God to work things out, or will we give in to the temptations offered by the evil one?

2. **Read James 1:13-15** and write it out.

a) Where does temptation come from?

b) Where does sin come from?

c) If we let sin have its way, what happens? Using the world around you, write down a couple of examples of sin's progression.

d) When are we more easily enticed by temptation?

e) Is there any place you are being enticed? If so, ask God what you are to do. Write down what comes to mind.

3. **Read Psalm 23**. Ask God to highlight one verse as encouragement for today. Write it down and then respond in a written prayer.

You will keep in perfect peace
him whose mind is steadfast, because he trusts in you.
—Isaiah 26:3

WEEK EIGHT
DAY TWO   REFLECT

The more we trust God, the more freedom we live in—the more joy, peace, patience, kindness, and love we can receive from God and give to others. No wonder the evil one wants to entice us away from trusting God, into taking things into our own hands.

1. Read Exodus 19:1-9. Let's look at Moses and the Israelites to see the tactics the evil one used then and continues to use today.
    a) What was God's promise?

    b) How did the people respond?

    c) How did God intend to provide for the people (see verse 9)?

2. Most of Exodus chapters 20-31 record God's directions to Moses for the people.
    a) **Read Exodus 20:18-21**. What was the purpose of God's testing?

    b) **Read Exodus 24:18**. How long was Moses on the mountain?

3. **Read Exodus 32:1-24**. The Holy Spirit was not given to believers until after Jesus' resurrection. People were dependent on God-appointed men to tell them what God was saying and doing. As we have read, Moses was God's provision for the Israelites at this time.
    a) What was the pressure the people felt?

    b) What pressure did Aaron feel?

c) Trying to relieve the pressure, what did the people grasp?

d) Ask God if you have recently given into pressure and grasped something other than what he had for you.

4. The evil one has all kinds of schemes to deceive us. Looking at the Israelites' responses to the test or pressures they were experiencing, write the corresponding tactic used by the enemy.

Israelites' Response to Testing

___ A. We have been waiting so long.

___ B. Moses is not coming back. We're on our own.

___ C. God must not really care about us.

___ D. We don't have anything to worship, and things aren't like we thought they would be.

___ E. We'll go with Plan B and make an idol. We can figure this out on our own.

___ F. Maybe we're not a treasured people or a holy nation; we must not be special, after all.

Enemy's Tactics

1. gets us to question our identity

2. speaks to our pride and capability

3. looks for an opportune time

4. causes us to question God's goodness

5. brings in fear to twist our perception

6. gets us to focus on the negative and what we lack

5. **Pray:** *Father God, I am sometimes like the Israelites. The enemy's tactic that most often trips me up is:*

In that place, forgive me for believing this lie:

What is your truth?

Thank you. Strengthen me to live in the truth today. In Jesus' name, Amen.

> So be careful to do what the Lord your God has commanded you; do not turn aside to the right or to the left.
> —Deuteronomy 5:3

WEEK EIGHT
DAY THREE   REFLECT

Is it sometimes confusing to you, knowing God could easily remove the pressures in your life? Yet God knows us so well, he understands what it will take for us to trust him more fully. The more we trust God, the less power the evil one will have over us.

As parents, when our little ones pull themselves up and then stand on their own, it is not too long before we are holding out our hands and coaxing, "Come to Mommy. Take a step. It's okay, I'm here to hold onto." We want to help our children walk on their own; we don't want them to be babies forever.

> *The more we trust God, the less power the evil one will have over us.*

In the same way, God challenges us so that we can grow in our faith. There is great gain in trusting him—in not leaning on our own understanding. We receive peace. And the amount of peace we experience

126

seems to correlate to our degree of trust in God.

Knowing this, will you look at pressures in your life differently? Will you look at them as opportunities to know God more fully? Pressures allow your heart to be tested, purified, and refined so that you might live more like Jesus lived.

1. Read Psalm 26:2 and Psalm 139:23-24.
   a) Write them down.

   b) Ask God how it benefits you to have him reveal your hidden motives and character. Write down what you hear.

2. a) In what place in your life do you feel pressure?

   b) How might this be a test of your trust in God?

   c) Ask God how the evil one might try to tempt you in the midst of this.

   d) Ask God what you have to gain by waiting on and trusting him.

3. **Read 1 Corinthians 10:13 and Hebrews 2:18.** Using these verses, write a prayer thanking God for his compassion and provision in the midst of pressure and tests.

Perhaps God is saying to you: *This life circumstance is going to test your faith, but have no fear; I will lead you. I don't want you to avoid it, to ignore it, or to minimize it. I will lead you through. And you will come out of the test with more trust in me than you have today. Yes, the evil one will try to get you to believe it is too much to handle. He will try to get you to grasp things that will relieve the pressure temporarily or to believe lies about me. Stay focused. I will provide a way out.*

WEEK EIGHT
DAY FOUR   REFLECT

Moses and the Israelites had seen God work supernaturally over and over. The Red Sea had been parted so they could pass through on dry land; manna and quail were provided by God in the desert; and they had been led on the exodus by a pillar of clouds during the day and a pillar of fire at night. Yet they got into another tough situation and forgot God could be trusted. Are we so different?

There were consequences to their forgetfulness and doubts. For example, instead of an eleven day journey to the Promised Land, the Israelites wandered around the desert for forty years. And after all that time, Moses was not allowed in. Let's look at another example of consequences from the Exodus scriptures.

1. **Read Exodus 32:15–20 and 34:1-4.** What was the cost of disobedience to Moses and the Israelites?

2. The consequences of giving in to temptation and fear are great. Once again, we see how God has made provision for us to live trusting him in the midst of pressure. **Read I Chronicles 16:8–12 and Hebrews 12:1,2.** List at least five tools we have for avoiding the enticement of temptation.

KINGDOM LAB:
Rather than putting our trust in God and focusing on him, we often shift our focal point to other things:

- finances	- friends	- career/success
- health	- retirement	- leisure activities
- family	- appearance	- church responsibilities

These can then become places of pressure or tests for us.

Pray:

• *Holy Spirit, come. I want to hear your voice, your counsel, your wisdom.* (Wait until you sense his presence. You may want to pray: *I bind distractions in the name of Jesus Christ.*)

• *Lord, search my mind and heart. Show me what I'm often focused on instead of you.* (It may be helpful to picture yourself looking at a blank screen. Ask God to bring whatever you're focusing on across the screen.)

• *What is the warning to me? What is the temptation I may fall into if this continues to be my focus?*

• *What does this area of my life look like with you as my focus?*

• *Have I forgotten what I've seen you do before in this area of my life or how I've seen you show up?*

• **Fill-in-the-blanks:**
Forgive me, Lord, *for forgetting what I've seen you do, for focusing on* _____ *instead of you.*

Forgive me for _____
_____ .

Thank you for the truth _____
_____ .

• *How will I keep my focus on you? What tools do you want me to use?*

• *How will you strengthen me?*

• *Thank you, Lord that you nudge me and invite me to grow in faith and in trusting you. It's what I want. Be persistent. I desire your help. Deliver me from the evil one. In Jesus' name, Amen.*

WEEK EIGHT
DAY FIVE
A familiar knock on the door brought me in from the balcony of my room. "Are you out there?" I called.

"Yes, I'm a little *out-there*, but you can trust me," Josh teased as I opened the door.

Evening was casting its shadows on the mountains as Josh joined me on the balcony chairs. The final petition of the Lord's Prayer had impacted me, and I'd realized countless ways I'd given into life's pressures—compromised my integrity to please a friend, spent money I didn't have because I needed a lift, replayed conversations in my mind rather than praying—totally missing out on learning to trust God.

"From now on when I pray through the Lord's Prayer, I'm going to stop and ask God if he has any warnings for me—any way I might be tempted to take things into my own hands to temporarily relieve pressure.

"One more thing, Josh. I'm going to ask God to remind me of ways he's shown up in similar circumstances so I'll have faith he'll show up again."

"Do you think you'll look at stressful situations and relationships differently now?" Josh questioned.

"I realize the test God has for me in those places is, 'Will I trust him? Will I not be anxious or afraid?' I don't have to worry about figuring out a solution. I want to do what God asks and trust him to deliver me, defend me, or provide for me—in his timing."

"How does that make you feel, Taylor?"

"Free." I let that soak in. "I feel free."

Just as I said the word free, an eagle soared by. *Thank you, God.*

"Taylor, yesterday when you thought about going home this morning, whose idea do you think that was?"

"I was just being practical—wanting to use God's money wisely."

"Did you ask God, or did you presume that's what he would want?"

Josh's question went right to my heart, "I guess I just presumed." *Will I ever figure this out?* "But God's all about being thrifty, isn't he?"

"Do you think he would have wanted you to miss out on spending today here?"

"What I've learned since this morning has been amazing. I've gained truth about God as well as experienced his character and love. I guess presumption can be a three letter word: sin."

> *One more way the evil one sneaks into my life... with good ideas. Help! I'm desperate for God.*

"Your reasons for leaving sounded good—even noble and self-sacrificing. But maybe you were using your wisdom, not God's."

"One more way the evil one sneaks into my life...with good ideas. Help! I'm desperate for God."

"That's a good place to be. And another good place would be dinner. Are you ready to go?"

As Josh and I walked down the hall, I again heard the whirring sound coming from behind one of the doors, and finally remembered to ask him about it.

"This would be a great time for me to show you, Taylor. I think you'll understand."

Josh opened the door, and I saw a huge stainless steel machine with large spools of thread on spindles up and down one side. They seemed to feed into the machine.

"Come around to the other side," Josh said. A tapestry was coming out from a slot in the machine, its movement undetectable to me. Josh took the wide tube it was rolled on and began unrolling it. From my point of view, it looked like a mess—threads and strings going every which way. Then Josh held up the other side for me to see.

I was caught off-guard and let out an exclamation of, "Wow!" No words in my vocabulary were enough for the exquisite piece of artwork, the intricacy of design, and the depth of colors and light. As I looked more carefully, I saw a glimmering fish, an archway and cross, and—was that the firebox?—woven into the pattern. I stood in silence. Josh understood. And when I could, I said, "Tell me about it."

"This is a computerized loom. It takes data from our guest list, our prayer requests and praise reports, and our guest comment cards and somehow assigns each one a color, length, and place in the overall design—weaves it together—and this is what we end up with. If we were to cut an inch long section out, it wouldn't make sense. But as you stand back, the inches fit together and make a beautiful tapestry story.

"Taylor, we have a whole other life that is being woven by God in the spiritual realm. We can only see it partially through the lens of the Holy

Spirit—but it is real. There is another reality you can't necessarily explain, but you can experience."

"Josh, I'm not sure I'm quite getting it, but something that's happened the past few days is making sense. Several times you reminded me of someone—my grandmother, a teacher, a swim instructor, my youth leader—it was so real, I thought you had to be related to them.

"They all knew Jesus and were *kingdom residents,* as you call it. It's as if what they have and what you have are woven together—interconnected somehow."

"That's great insight, Taylor. God's plan to redeem the world and to make himself known is woven into every Christ-follower. As we grow in our faith, we become more like him. As he forgives, we forgive; as he serves, we serve; as he loves, we love.

"We're unique individuals—different parts of the body of Christ—with different stories, yet interwoven for a purpose far greater than we can see."

"Thanks, Josh. I keep thinking everything I experience or learn is the absolute best—and then there's more."

"That's the way it is in the kingdom of God, Taylor; always more to experience with the King. What a great lead-in for the banquet. Let's go."

My head was spinning. I felt like my brain would burst if I didn't stop and process some of what was happening to me. On my way out, I paused at the spools of tapestry thread, and the silliest grin came over my face. Of course Josh caught it and gave me the "what now?" look.

"I was just wondering what color the trout and zucchini principle might be."

Then a metallic gold and silver thread caught my eye and I pointed to it. Looking at

> *God's plan to redeem the world and to make himself known is woven into every Christ-follower.*

Josh I said, "This is the thread I'd use for your gift of friendship to me. I hope someday someone says to me, 'There's something about you that reminds me of a friend I had. His name was Josh.' Thank you, Josh. I'm so glad I came."

REFLECT

1. Read 1 Corinthians 2:9-16.

a) Ask God for three or four thoughts from these verses that tie into Taylor's revelations at The Father's House.

1.

2.

3.

4.

b) How is truth from the Bible discerned?

c) Write down one encouragement or challenge to you from this Scripture passage.

2. **Read 1 Chronicles 29:10-13**, part of King David's prayer. The early church added, "For yours is the kingdom, and the power, and the glory for ever and ever. Amen," to the Lord's Prayer. It was probably taken from these verses. What other attributes of God are listed in this passage?

3. **Read 1 Chronicles 29:20**. If you are physically able, kneel or lay on the floor (prostrate before the Lord) and pray through the Lord's Prayer. Pray slowly, listening to the Lord, adding to the prayer the things the Lord puts on your heart. End in praise with the assurance that your Heavenly Father knows you, provides for you, and loves you. Write down your experience.

For his is the Kingdom, and the Power, and the Glory for Ever and Ever. Amen

Epilogue

The next morning, driving down the road from The Father's House, I relived my experience. *How could so much have happened in just a few days?* I was going home a different person than when I'd arrived—no, not with a new identity in the natural realm, but in the spiritual realm I realized I was a kingdom resident. I was in the process of being made more Christ-like every day.

The banquet the night before was not only a feast, but a celebration. I'd met people I knew I'd see again and already had plans to bring my mom and dad for an adult family weekend retreat. *I hope they'll want to come.*

A Communion service in the chapel followed dinner. I was sure I'd have to stand up and be acknowledged for designing the firebox and Communion table, but nothing was mentioned. I have to admit I felt a twinge of disappointment, but then great freedom washed over me. What I had done was no more valuable than what the dishwashers had done after the banquet. I liked kingdom living.

Communion was a rededication service for me. Through Josh's example and friendship, I had a new understanding of what Jesus had done for me on the cross. Before I went up to the Communion table, I stopped by the firebox and left my fear of darkness and a couple more resentments that had come to mind. Something about seeing them burn felt freeing to me.

As we ate the bread and drank the wine, my heart overflowed with gratefulness. I had come to The Father's House—I had come for awhile, just as he had asked—and I'd met my heavenly Father in real ways. Now I'd meet with my heavenly Father every day, anywhere I was. The Father's House was woven into me through the Holy Spirit.

The sun began to peek over the mountains, and I reached for my sunglasses. *Not above the visor.* I pulled over and checked the glove box, and then my bag. *"Where are they, God?"* I prayed. A picture of the balcony table in my room at The Father's House came to mind, and I turned around.

At least this time I know how to find the entrance. Several people were wandering around the grounds of The Father's House—some praying in the garden alcoves, some visiting, and some pruning trees and bushes.

I walked to the office and asked if I could go upstairs and get my sunglasses. Sure enough, they were still on the balcony table and I took in a last visual gulp of the scenery. *Thank you, Father.*

Walking down the hall, the sound of whirring caused me to pause outside the tapestry room. *There's time for one more glance.* I opened the door. The sound grew louder, but why? *Where is the loom?* All I saw was a spool of gold and silver thread on a small table against the wall. *Gold and silver? Josh must have something to do with this.* As I picked up the spool, a handwritten note became visible:

> *Now the Lord is the Spirit, and where the Spirit of the Lord is,*
> *there is freedom. And we, who with unveiled faces all reflect the*
> *Lord's glory, are being transformed into his likeness with ever-*
> *increasing glory, which comes from the Lord, who is the Spirit.*
> —2 Corinthians 3:17-18

I glanced out the window. *Just when I think I've got it figured out, I realize there's so much I don't understand. What had Josh said? "There's a whole other reality you can't explain but you can experience."*

Setting the thread down, I went back to the office. *I've got to ask Josh about this.*

"Could you tell me where I can find Josh?" I asked the receptionist.

"Josh? Is he a guest here?"

"No, he's the gardener—for plants and souls—you must know him."

"We haven't ever had anyone on staff named Josh. You're sure that's his name?"

This reality thing was getting even more mystifying. *If there's no Josh, what about my bill?* "Would you mind checking to see if anything's due on my bill? I forgot to ask before I left."

"Sure Taylor. Just a minute."

The receptionist pulled a file, looked it over and said, "Your balance due is zero. I hope you'll be back again soon."

"I know this is a bizarre question, but how was it paid?"

Shrugging her shoulders, she answered, "It doesn't say. Hey, could you use any zucchini? They just brought some extra in from the greenhouse."

Thank you for joining us on this journey through the Lord's Prayer. May we continue to follow Jesus, being led by the Holy Spirit, drawing near to our heavenly Father, and loving him and one another.

Resources

Barker, Stephen G., Pastor Emeritus, First Presbyterian Church, Yakima, WA. Personal interview. 2010.

The Holy Bible. New International Version. Grand Rapids, MI: Zondervan,1986.

Johnson, Darrell W., *Fifty-Seven Words that Change the World,* Vancouver, British Columbia: Regent College Publishing, 2005.

McReynolds, Paul R., *Word Study Greek-English New Testament,* Wheaton, Illinois: Tyndale House Publishers, Inc., 1999.

Strong, James, *Strong's Exhaustive Concordance of the Bible,* Peabody, MA: Hendrickson Publishers, 2007.

Unger, Merrill F., *The New Unger's Bible Dictionary,* Chicago, Illinois: Moody Press, 1988.

Webster, Noah, *American Dictionary of the English Language (1828),* San Francisco, CA: American Christian History Education Series, Fifteenth printing, May 2002.

About the Authors

Kathy Bricel and Kathy Myers have been team-teaching a Bible study, *Living a Spirit Led Life*, since 2004. In the midst of studying the Scriptures, they have discovered the joy of learning to hear and discern God's voice, and they have a passion to share it with others.

Kathy Bricel is married to Jim and has three grown sons and a beautiful daughter-in-law. She serves as the co-director for SOAR: School of Spiritual Transformation. Kathy and Jim are involved with Living Waters for the World, where they help install water filtration systems and bring the message of the Gospel to those in need of clean water. They are also part of a teaching staff that trains and equips others to do the same.

Kathy Myers is married to Dick and has two married sons. She is enjoying the addition of delightful daughters-in-law and grandchildren to her life. Kathy and Dick have served on the local Young Life committee for many years, helping bring the good news of Jesus Christ to teens in the Yakima Valley.

The Kathys have written several Bible studies and taught at retreats. They find joy in seeing people come into freedom and wholeness through prayer. In their pursuit of God and love of family, friends, and community, they find life a joy-filled adventure. Contact them through: www.livingaspiritledlife.com

---

Special thanks to our friend and Holy Spirit-infused encourager, Nancy Gustafson, who has been with us every step of the way. She represents many others who have come alongside us with feedback and encouragement. We are grateful for the blessing of living in community.

CPSIA information can be obtained at www.ICGtesting.com
Printed in the USA
LVOW12s2154190913

353295LV00005B/218/P